AUSTSWIM.®

Teaching Infant and Preschool Aquatics

Water Experiences the Australian Way

Contributors

Judy Cesari	Ross Gage
Meredith King	Jenni Maclean
Julie Zancanaro	Christine Ure

Nell White

Illustrated by

Mary Ann Hurley

Library of Congress Cataloging-in-Publication Data

Teaching infant and preschool aquatics / contributing authors, Judy Cesari, Ross Gage, Meredith King ... [et al.]; illustrated by Mary Ann Hurley.
    p. cm.
  ISBN 0-7360-3250-9
  1. Swimming for infants--Study and teaching. 2. Swimming for children--Study and teaching. 3. Swimming--Safety measures. I. Cesari, Judy. II. Gage, Ross. III. King, Meredith. IV. AUSTSWIM Inc.

GV837.25.T42 2000
797.2'1'083--dc21

                                                                00-044939

ISBN: 0-7360-3250-9

Copyright © 2001 by AUSTSWIM Inc.

This book is a revised edition of *Teaching Infant and Preschool Aquatics*, published in 1998 by AUSTSWIM Inc.

Managing Editors: Leigh LaHood and Laurie Stokoe; **Proofreader:** Sue Fetters; **Graphic Designer:** Nancy Rasmus; **Graphic Artist:** Brian McElwain; **Cover Designer:** Jack W. Davis; **Photographer and Illustrator:** Mary Ann Hurley; **Printer:** United Graphics

Human Kinetics books are available at special discounts for bulk purchase. Special editions or book excerpts can also be created to specification. For details, contact the Special Sales Manager at Human Kinetics.

Printed in the United States of America

10 9 8 7 6 5 4 3 2 1

Human Kinetics
Web site: www.humankinetics.com

United States: Human Kinetics
P.O. Box 5076
Champaign, IL 61825-5076
800-747-4457
e-mail: humank@hkusa.com

Canada: Human Kinetics
475 Devonshire Road Unit 100
Windsor, ON N8Y 2L5
800-465-7301 (in Canada only)
e-mail: hkcan@mnsi.net

Europe: Human Kinetics
P.O. Box IW14
Leeds LS16 6TR, United Kingdom
+44 (0)113 278 1708
e-mail: humank@hkeurope.com

Australia: Human Kinetics
57A Price Avenue
Lower Mitcham, South Australia 5062
08 8277 1555
e-mail: liahka@senet.com.au

New Zealand: Human Kinetics
P.O. Box 105-231, Auckland Central
09-309-1890
e-mail: hkp@ihug.co.nz

CONTENTS

FOREWORD

Swimming and water safety programs have changed significantly in recent years. There is an ever-increasing demand for quality instruction by competent teachers with specialised knowledge.

One significant change has been the increase in the number of infants and preschool children enrolled in aquatic activity programs by parents and caregivers. (AUSTSWIM has defined an infant as a child from birth to the age of 42 months and a preschooler as from 42 to 48 months.) With an increased number of infants and preschoolers participating in aquatic activity programs there has been a demand for appropriately qualified teachers. This manual has been developed as the prescribed reference publication for teachers undertaking the AUSTSWIM Teacher of Infant Aquatics certificate course. The publication is extremely valuable for all with an interest in the health and well-being of young children—particularly parents and caregivers.

I am impressed with the quality of the AUSTSWIM text. This book will confidently take AUSTSWIM into the new millennium with a further outstanding resource. The book will provide many swimming teachers and instructors with a valuable resource and can also be used as a reference again and again.

The easy-to-use format and the teaching hints and processes will ensure that many teachers, instructors or students will find that many questions that they may have are answered; they can be assured that the information is up to date and world leading.

AUSTSWIM is dedicated to developing the most up-to-date swimming teaching resources and will continue with the commitment to ensure that they remain at the forefront of swimming teaching today.

Kirk Marks
Chairman
September 1999

PUBLISHER'S PREFACE

The swimming programs developed by the Australian aquatics organisation AUSTSWIM are known throughout the world for their excellence. Those in the field of aquatics also recognize AUSTSWIM's instructor training for these successful programs as the yardstick for competency-based training. Human Kinetics is proud to offer this international edition of the AUSTSWIM manual *Teaching Infant and Preschool Aquatics*. Now instructor candidates everywhere can study it to develop the knowledge and skills they need to become proficient teachers of aquatics for young children. Parents also can learn more about appropriate aquatic activities for their children.

The manual begins with a chapter on the philosophy of aquatics for infants (from birth to 42 months) and preschoolers (from 42 to 48 months). It explains the purpose of aquatic programs for this age group and the roles of teachers and parents in such programs, and it provides guidelines for working with children at different ages. Infant health and safety in an aquatic environment is considered next, encompassing issues such as environmental safety, infants' and preschoolers' health, and resuscitation of infants and young children. Then the developmental stages of infants and young children are described, covering six stages of motor development, cognitive development and communication, and personal development for children from birth through the age of four. Chapter 4 lays out principles of teacher, parent, and child relationships in teaching aquatics. Methods of water familiarisation is the topic of chapter 5, which includes holding positions, floating, mobility in the water, submersion and breath control, entries and exits, and the use of flotation aids and water toys. The final chapter provides information on how to structure aquatic lessons for young children, along with sample songs and games.

Teaching Infant and Preschool Aquatics is an outstanding resource that instructors can refer to again and again. Its easy-to-use format and the teaching hints and processes it includes will answer many instructors' and parents' questions. Instructors can rely on this manual for the useful, up-to-date information they need.

ACKNOWLEDGMENTS

AUSTSWIM gratefully acknowledges the generous support provided by the Commonwealth Government of Australia through the National Office of Sport and Recreation Policy of the Department of Industry, Science and Tourism.

AUSTSWIM acknowledges the contributions made by the many people who have a special interest in infant and preschool aquatic activity programs especially Nell White (AQUATOTS-South Africa) and also those who have reviewed materials for the publication. Special thanks go to Richard Cahalan, Terese Gage, Debbie Marks, Kirk Marks, Judy Watts and Helen Wheatley.

INTRODUCTION

This book provides guidelines for the aquatic education of infants and preschool children. These guidelines have been designed to reflect stages in the developmental readiness of infants and preschool children for particular aquatic experiences and teaching methods. The book presents a comprehensive account of the developmental changes that characterize early development and the practical implications of these for teaching and learning. The information provided also addresses some of the controversial issues that have arisen in the arena of infant and preschool aquatic education, particularly philosophical and pedagogical issues concerning water safety and submersion. The roles that adults play in young children's early education are also explored.

When infant aquatic education is approached from a developmental philosophy, the personal, physical and cognitive needs of infants and young children will be respected and planned for. The teaching methods adopted for infant and preschool aquatic education will then encourage children's natural curiosity and desire to explore and learn through playful interaction with their parents, peers and teachers.

The AUSTSWIM Council advises all teachers, parents and pool management involved in infant and preschool aquatic programs of the following key points:

- Participation in aquatic activities should be an enjoyable experience for infants, preschoolers and their parents.
- Infants and preschoolers should be able to learn at their own pace and never be forced to be involved in water activities.
- Irrespective of their aquatic ability infants and preschoolers are never safe when in or around water and must be under constant *adult* supervision.

The AUSTSWIM Council further recommends that guidelines for infant and preschool aquatic programs be divided into the following categories. The age categories form a useful basis for planning, grouping practices and implementation.

Classification	Age Indicator	Performance	Ratio Indicator
Newborn	Birth to 6 months	Sensory exploration	With parent
Baby 1 and Baby 2	6-12 months 12-24 months	Water familiarisation and initial independence	1:1 parent/child 1:8 teacher/parent-child pairs
Toddler 1 and Toddler 2	24-36 months 36-42 months	Water familiarisation and basic skill development	1:8 teacher/parent-child pairs 1:4 teacher-children
Preschool	42-48 months	Confidence and basic aquatic skill development	1:5 teacher-children

The guidelines presented in this book are designed to assist both teachers and parents to conduct aquatic programs. Adults who work with young children are in a unique position to foster positive attitudes towards infants' and young children's early learning. It cannot be stressed too strongly that at no time does an infant's or preschooler's increased confidence and ability in the water eliminate the need for constant supervision by a competent adult while he or she is involved in aquatic activities or in the vicinity of water.

Chapter 1

PHILOSOPHY OF INFANT AND PRESCHOOL AQUATICS

Statement of Philosophy

Infant and preschool aquatic education programs are designed to assist infants, young children and parents in becoming familiar with the water and developing confidence in the water through participation in a range of safe and enjoyable aquatic activities. Fun activities may lead to the development of basic swimming and water safety skills through play, exploration and encouragement. The expectations of the program and the teaching methods used are appropriate for the stages of development and are designed to reflect the physical, social, emotional and intellectual competencies of infants and preschool children.

Teachers play an important role in shaping the lifestyle of children and families under their care. Educators who work with infants and very young children are in a privileged position, as they are often the first contact that young children and their families have with educational services. In aquatic programs this privileged position carries with it a high level of trust and responsibility, as parents are placing their infants and very young children under the guidance of a teacher in circumstances normally associated with a high level of risk.

Purpose of Aquatic Programs for Infants and Preschool Children

Infant and preschool aquatic programs are designed to do the following:

- Introduce parents and their infants and preschool children to routines and guidelines that promote safety in and around the water.
- Respect the human rights and dignity of infants and preschool children.
- Instruct parents in methods that will help infants and preschool children to be confident and happy in the water and willing to learn.
- Cater to a wide range of individual differences in infants and preschool children.
- Assist infants and preschool children to become familiar with the water.

- Promote water confidence at an early age.
- Introduce preliminary aquatic activities which, with maturation, patience, practice and time, may lead to the development of age-appropriate aquatic skills in infants and preschool children.
- Use methods of teaching that promote the physical, personal and intellectual well-being of infants and preschool children.
- Provide experiences that encourage infants and preschool children to return to the water eagerly and willingly.
- Provide opportunities for parents and young children to share in a social activity.

Definitions of Infants and Preschool Children

For the purposes of this book, the periods of infancy and early childhood are divided into a number of key stages that reflect the developmental characteristics of young children, as shown in this table.

Newborn	Birth to 6 months
Baby 1	6-12 months
Baby 2	12-24 months
Toddler 1	24-36 months
Toddler 2	36-42 months
Preschool	42-48 months

Characteristics of the Infant and Preschool Child at Each Key Stage

These key stages reflect changes in the motor skills, cognitive skills and the personal development of infants and preschool children. At each stage infants and children show characteristic motor, cognitive and personal developments that determine their ability to engage in aquatic programs and to learn from them. AUSTSWIM has used these characteristics to develop a program guide appropriate to infants at each key stage.

Motor development refers to aspects of posture and locomotion as well as manipulation, while *cognitive development* refers to changes in awareness and understanding of the world and daily events and patterns of communication. *Personal development* refers to changes in emotional needs and social competencies. The following section presents an outline of the developmental characteristics of infants and preschoolers across these domains from birth to 48 months of age. A more detailed explanation of these developments and the implications for working with infants and young children in aquatic activities is given in chapter 3.

Newborn Stage (Birth to 6 Months)

Motor development: Movements are governed by over 70 different reflexes and general writhing movements. Infants have limited head control and self-regulated movement.

Cognitive development: Learns through sensory exploration and repetition. Makes limited associations between action and reaction. Communicates through crying and non-verbal cues.

Personal development: Accepts strangers, although selective responses to parents.

Newborns depend on their parents for play and social activity.

This period is characterised by reflex control of the body, particularly during the first three months of life. Reflexes regulate infants' responses to stimuli and they operate automatically; for example, the hand closes and grasps an object that is placed against the palm. Reflexes govern all types of movement, including posture and locomotor responses. In the water infants will display a swimming reflex and on land they will demonstrate a stepping reflex.

Self-initiated control over posture and locomotion begins to emerge in the second half of this period (4-6 months) as infants gain control over the posture and movements of the upper body. In the aquatic environment newborns are buoyant but unable to control their own movements. During the first 3 months their involvement in the water is largely passive and they are engaged in a sensory experience.

From about 4 months infants become more active participants but do not have the organised motor control to move independently in the water and adapt their responses. Social and emotional behaviour during this stage is characterised by dependence on the parent. Infants will learn to trust new and unfamiliar situations when their parents are responsive to their needs.

Baby 1 Stage (6-12 Months)

Motor development: Voluntary movement, postural control of upper body leading to upright posture for sitting and standing and good manipulative control.

Cognitive development: Early exploration. Memory and anticipation. Cries and vocalises.

Personal development: Sensitive to emotions and expressions of others. Resistant to strangers.

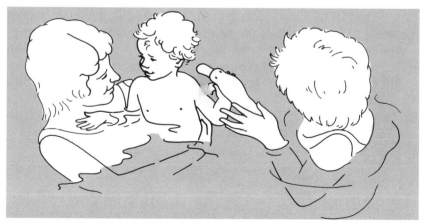

Six- to 12-month-old infants need their parents for reassurance.

Infants establish control over their posture and movements, commencing with the upper body. They are buoyant in the water but may begin to resist floating on their backs, as they tend to roll and become upright. They love to explore their environment, reach and grasp toys and splash the water for an effect. The emergence of the ability to remember enables infants in this age range to begin to anticipate events and to engage in simple games such as 'Peek-a-boo' and 'Clap Hands'. They can also begin to learn the early stages of breath-holding through remembering and associating cues that help prepare for submersion. They are very sensitive to emotional expression and often express 'stranger anxiety'. They may strongly resist being handled by anyone other than their parents.

Baby 2 Stage (12-24 Months)

Motor development: Upright. Walking. Automatic control. Able to use hands with some refinement and pick objects up and place them down.

Cognitive development: A period of exploration. Relates cause and effect. Remembers and associates people and events etc. Understands more than she or he can say.

Personal development: Returns to parent for support. Emerging independence begins to result in conflicts.

Infants have now established good control over their posture and at the end of this period can walk well and begin to run. Increased motor control provides them with more opportunities to explore on their own, and they love to test out cause and effect with objects and actions. In the aquatic environment they cope best when they can touch a surface with their feet. They may become successful in independent entry and exit and may begin to propel themselves through the water. A wide range of skills can be mastered during this stage. Their level of understanding is developing and they want to try things out. This is an emotionally difficult time, particularly from about 18 to 24 months, as infants attempt to establish self-control. They often appear wilful, as they lack the ability to see other people's point of view.

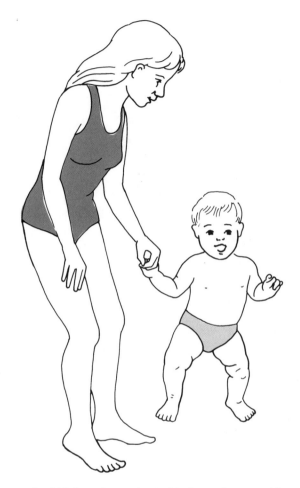

Twelve- to 24-month-old infants have physical independence and love to explore. They return to their parents frequently for reassurance.

Toddler 1 Stage (24-36 Months)

Motor development: Walks and runs automatically. Beginning to coordinate the whole body in a more unified way.

Cognitive development: Good vocabulary, but a limited ability to understand the perspectives of others. Communication skills are expanding through a wider vocabulary.

Personal development: Plays alone alongside others. More independent and begins to relate to the teacher more.

Toddlers love to be near others, although they do not have the sophisticated social skills needed for group play.

Toddlers begin to adapt their movement skills and organise them into more coordinated patterns that involve integration of the whole body. In the aquatic environment their self-propulsion is more efficient and they begin to coordinate this with breath control. They are highly independent, persistent and may not always comply easily. Routines help them predict what will happen and promote a stable environment. At this stage they need opportunity to show what they can do. They enjoy the company of their peers and seek them out but do not play with them in a highly interactive manner. They tend to play alongside their peers rather than talk and interact. They are imaginative and love fantasy play.

Toddler 2 Stage (36-42 Months)

Motor development: Coordinated and tries out new skills, e.g. walks with a rhythmical gait, swings the arms in opposition to the legs.

Cognitive development: Talks in sentences. Has a sense of time and a good memory for events and detail. Communicates in sentences.

Personal development: Egocentric, although beginning to understand others' perspectives more. Able to interact with peers more successfully.

By age 3, toddlers begin to understand the needs of others and engage more successfully in group play.

Toddlers can now organise their movements into more complex patterns such as those needed for galloping and hopping, and show more rhythmical organisation. They are able to propel themselves successfully through the water and coordinate limb movements with their breathing in early patterns for swimming. The behaviour of toddlers at this stage is more relaxed and autonomous. Toddlers in this age group are beginning to negotiate and reason, although their limited capacity for personal understanding and language and their tendency to focus on one aspect of a situation make them appear one-sided and dogmatic.

Preschool Stage (42-48 Months)

Motor development: Walks in an adult manner. Runs with control and increasing stride. Hops and skips. Can master a range of skills, e.g. ride a bike, with good balance.

Cognitive development: Understands stories and is highly imaginative. Likes to know how things work or happen. Communicates by asking questions and often uses speech to initiate actions.

Personal development: Able to play in groups. The ability to see others' perspectives is developing but tends to consider only one aspect at a time. Works well with simple rules.

Preschoolers are active and energetic and love to try out new skills.

Preschool children move well and have more rhythmical movements characterised by greater integration of the whole body. Walking, running and jumping are all showing mature characteristics. Some children can hop. These movements are supported through cross-lateral integration of the limbs and the arms swing in opposition to the legs. These movements provide a good foundation for the development of swimming strokes, which also require cross-lateral coordination. Children in this age group still think about their world in concrete ways. They tend to focus on one aspect of a situation and be egocentric. These characteristics limit their ability to see a problem from different viewpoints. They have good language skills and enjoy fantasy and group interaction. Their responses to situations lack adaptability and they tend to judge situations simply as right or wrong, or good or bad.

It is important to note that these characteristics are general descriptions for each stage and that all children are individuals. Each infant's development will be influenced by a variety of factors, including differences in rates of development, differences in personality and prior experiences. It must also be appreciated that children who enter an aquatic program for the first time will need time to adjust to the water-based environment and may appear less skilled in the water than children of the same age who have had more experience.

The Roles of the Teacher, Parent, Infant and Preschooler

The Teacher (Skilled Adviser and Facilitator)

The infant and preschool aquatics teacher's role is to provide knowledge and support for parents and to demonstrate, through an effective program, appropriate methods of teaching infants and preschool children. The aquatics teacher should respect the special relationship between infants and their parents and understand that parents are an infant's first and most important teachers. Teachers should provide the knowledge and skills to assist parents to

Roles of the teacher, parent and infant.

- learn about the development of their infants and preschool children;
- understand which aquatic experiences are appropriate at different stages of development;
- feel competent with infants and preschoolers in the water;
- understand the importance of playful interactions in learning;
- develop strategies for introducing infants and young children to new experiences in a positive and nonthreatening manner;
- interact socially with other parents and children of similar ages and stages of development through group experiences; and
- appreciate their responsibility for the water safety of infants and preschool children.

The teacher facilitates and helps parents to
- enjoy their infant,
- understand their infant's development,
- hold and move their infant confidently in the water,
- learn how to promote their infant's aquatic skill development,
- value play in learning,
- create a relaxed and happy atmosphere,
- promote their child's self-esteem and competence, and
- be aware of their responsibility for their infant's water safety.

Parents support and teach their infant by
- praising and encouraging their infant,
- promoting a sense of trust and security,
- being realistic in their expectations of their infant's abilities in the water,
- modelling new skills,
- providing assistance and physical support as needed,
- helping their infant participate in small-group activities, and
- taking responsibility for their infant's water safety whenever he or she is in or near water.

The infant learns aquatic skills through
- having a sense of safety and security,
- being a relaxed and happy participant,
- play and exploration,
- feeling safe and secure when trying out new activities,
- believing that 'I can do it',
- participating in small-group activities,
- being able to try out new activities when she or he feels ready to try, and
- participating in regular routines that promote safe habits in and around water.

The Parents (Supporters and Teachers)

Parents are children's first teachers. Parents provide the emotional support infants need in order to feel secure. In the first year of life infants' primary attachment is to their parents. In the second year toddlers begin to move away from their parents and explore on their own. However, they do not move far away and return frequently to their parents for reassurance. By the third year toddlers are more autonomous and parents may begin to step back a little. During the fourth and fifth years children feel competent to participate in small-group situations with their teacher.

The aquatic program should help parents to

- appreciate their young child's need for support and security,
- share time with their infant or preschool child in a relaxed atmosphere,
- establish an early pattern of engagement in a physical recreational activity with their infant,
- help their child interact within small-group settings,
- appreciate how infants and preschool children acquire new skills and competencies,
- develop realistic expectations of infants and preschool children in aquatic programs, and
- appreciate the limited abilities of infants and young children in water and the need to maintain constant vigilance when children are in or near water.

The Infant and Preschool Child (the Learner)

The aquatic experience provides infants and preschool children with a new learning environment which has many benefits. It is important the methods of water familiarisation used in a program help infants gain a sense of their own competence. The infant aquatic program should provide infants and young children with the opportunity to

- enjoy sensory and motor experiences that are appropriate to each stage of development,
- learn through play and exploration of the aquatic environment,
- learn in a secure and relaxed atmosphere,
- engage in a regular physical activity in the company of others,

- gradually develop skills and competence for independence in the aquatic environment through experiences that are appropriate to each stage of development,
- develop a sense of their own autonomy in the aquatic environment,
- enjoy group activities and learning with others, and
- gain skills that may promote water safety in a manner that is appropriate for each stage of development.

Water Safety

The water safety of any person is dependent on that person's

- awareness of danger,
- sense of responsibility for self and others, and
- skills for survival and rescue.

Water safety is always the responsibility of adults when caring for infants and preschool children. Young children cannot be expected to take responsibility for their own safety or the safety of others. Infants and preschool children can be taught elements of survival skills such as rolling and floating. However, they cannot be expected to have sufficient awareness to protect themselves from danger or to transfer their skills from secure and structured situations to circumstances involving trauma. Infants and young children are particularly unsafe near water and roads. They fail to take in all the circumstances associated with an event and may be attracted to a key feature. For example, an infant may be attracted to a ball floating on water or rolling on the road, yet fail to appreciate the danger of falling into water or being hit by a car.

Infants who have many happy experiences in water may be more confident and less suspicious of water. Statistics on infant drowning show that infants under 4 years of age are at greatest risk of drowning. Adults who care for infants must have realistic expectations and understand that while infants are capable of learning some aspects of water safety and may be able to manage themselves in water in class situations, they cannot be considered to be water-safe without constant supervision.

Infants are not safe because they are often captivated by a single feature of an event and do not see the 'big picture'.

Guidelines for Infants and Preschoolers

These guidelines have been adopted by AUSTSWIM for advice to parents, teachers and pool management. The guidelines outline the conditions for infant aquatics education.

Newborn Stage (Birth to 6 Months)

We do not recommend formal aquatic programs for infants under 6 months of age. During this period parents should be given advice on how to use the family bath to introduce infants in the newborn stage to appropriate aquatic experiences at home and to prepare them for an infant aquatic program. Where aquatic programs for infants less than six months of age are conducted in public swimming pools care must be taken to ensure the health needs of infants are adequately met through a consideration of

- water hygiene,
- water and air temperature,
- handling techniques, and
- programming.

Baby 1 and 2 Stages (6-24 Months)

1. Infants participating in aquatic activity programs in a communal pool should be at least 6 months old.

Infants should be properly supported to prevent water swallowing. Water intoxication is a health risk to infants. Teachers and parents should be conscious of how much water an infant has ingested and remove the infant from the water if her or his stomach appears to become distended.

2. Aquatic programs for infants under the age of 24 months should be promoted as water familiarisation (getting used to the water).

Other terms such as 'drownproofing', 'waterproofing' or 'water-safe' should not be used, as they suggest some sort of guarantee. Parents must supervise their infants carefully at all times when they are in or near water. Emphasis should be placed on a happy, non-threatening, secure atmosphere which will provide for infants' social, intellectual, physical and emotional development.

3. Water familiarisation programs must involve both the education of parents and their in-water participation.

As primary educators, parents must assume responsibility for the supervision and learning of their infants. Programs should involve communicating safety rules, goals, techniques and expectations of infant aquatic education activities to parents.

4. Parents must ensure that their infants are in good health while participating in aquatic programs.

Pertinent health information about pre-existing conditions should be obtained from parents before an infant is accepted into the program. Teachers and parents need to be aware that physical and emotional health varies, from time to time, in each individual. Pre-existing medical and health conditions of parents should also be recorded.

5. Teachers conducting infant aquatic programs must be certified.

Teachers should have specific training in infant development, aquatic implications and how infants learn. Teachers should display an understanding, aptitude, patience and enthusiasm for this age group and continue their education to stay current with new developments. The teacher in the water and at least one other person present should have a current certificate in cardiopulmonary resuscitation (CPR) of infants and children.

6. Infants must be permitted to learn at their own rate. The number of participants in a class should allow for close supervision and individual attention.

Programs that include movement exploration and development, games and parent involvement in various land and water activities are appropriate. Development of specific skills in aquatics should not take precedence over infants' enjoyment of the water, but should be seen in relation to their overall development.

Infants should be taught using a parent-infant ratio of one to one. Classes should have a maximum of eight students. The key to learning is the emphasis placed on a positive environment working towards aquatic safety and enjoyment.

7. Only procedures and techniques that are age-appropriate, non-traumatic and respect the rights of the child are to be implemented. At no stage should force be used.

Infants must be properly supported to prevent the swallowing of water. Techniques such as throwing the infant into water from a height to force back floating are not recommended. Only when infants can demonstrate competent learnt response breath control can submersions be initiated. These submersions should initially be brief and few in number. Once infants can consistently initiate submersions and demonstrate competent breath control, these can become longer and more frequent. These experiences should be free of force, punishment or threat.

8. In-water class times should not exceed 30 minutes for infants.

Frequent, short learning experiences are best. Infants should not become cold and tired. Children who display signs of lost body heat should be immediately removed from the water, dried, kept warm and clothed.

9. The water temperature should be at least 30 degrees Celsius (86 degrees Fahrenheit) and ideally the air temperature should be higher.

This provides for optimum learning comfort and enjoyment. Infants become cold very quickly, so parents should wrap their infant in a towel when he or she is out of the water. The learning of aquatic skills should never take precedence over a child's comfort.

10. The pool facilities should be maintained according to standards specified by state and local authorities regarding safety, water purity and sanitary conditions.

Floors and passageways should be safe and have appropriate wet-area flooring. Dressing-rooms and changing tables should be well maintained.

11. Appropriate clothing should be worn by infants, parents and teachers.

Infants should wear pants that fit snugly around the legs to ensure that faeces do not enter the pool. Any infant having a bowel movement should leave the water and be washed and changed into clean clothing. Nappies or diapers are not suitable attire for aquatic activities. When infants may be exposed to the sun for potentially harmful periods, attention should be given to hats, sun clothes and sunscreen.

Toddler 1 and 2 Stages (24-42 Months)

Infants in this age group are becoming capable of learning basic aquatic techniques. Emphasis should be placed upon parental understanding. Ideally programs should be centred upon skill development and water safety education based on play, games and activities.

1. It is essential that parents understand the rationale for any formal aquatic program for their infants.

Programs that include movement exploration, water adjustment, fun, games and parent-infant involvement are appropriate for this age group. Development of specific skills in aquatics should not take precedence over the toddler's general well-being. Rather they should be seen in relation to overall development.

2. Parents are responsible for ensuring that the toddler is in good health while he or she is participating in aquatic programs.

Pertinent health information about existing conditions should be obtained from the parents before a toddler is accepted into a program. Teachers and parents need to be aware that physical and emotional health varies, from time to time, in each individual. Pre-existing medical and health conditions of parents should also be recorded.

3. Teachers conducting toddler aquatic programs must be certified.

Teachers should have specific training in infant development, aquatic implications and how infants learn. Teachers should display an understanding, aptitude, patience and enthusiasm for this age group. Teachers should continue their education to stay current with new developments. The teacher in the water and at least one other person present should have a current certificate in CPR of children and infants.

4. The teacher-pupil ratio should be low to take into account the needs of the toddlers.

Initially the toddlers will require the in-water participation of a parent. At around 36 months some infants may be ready to move into a transitional group without in-water participation of parents. This will depend upon their social and emotional development and aquatic readiness. A maximum teacher-pupil ratio of 1:5 allows for appropriate supervision and competent instruction.

5. The pool and associated facilities should be maintained according to standards laid down by state and local authorities regarding water purity and general sanitary conditions. Water temperature should be a minimum of 30 degrees Celsius; air temperature should be comparable.

Toddlers require optimum conditions for learning aquatic skills and minimal risk of infection when participating in aquatic programs.

6. Acceptable flotation aids may assist with the gaining of confidence and skill development.

Numerous teaching aids may improve the quality of aquatic programs but should only be used in controlled teaching situations. Flotation aids attached to the body are not lifesaving devices and should only be used under competent adult supervision. Such flotation aids must be acceptable to the Australian Standard 'Flotation Aids for Water Familiarisation and Swimming Tuition' or other local, state or national standards.

7. Rules of behaviour for activity in or near water should be taught as an integral element of the aquatic program.

Irrespective of aquatic ability, no toddler should be considered water-safe. Infants should learn from the earliest lesson how to behave when in or near water. Infants should be supervised at all times.

8. The learning of skills by the toddler is directly related to active participation in programs and frequency of practice.

The retention of skills is dependent upon reinforcement. These experiences should be free of force, punishment or threat.

9. Toddlers should be treated as individuals and allowed to progress at their own rate.

It is essential that teachers and parents understand the fears of toddlers and their need for reassurance and encouragement. Trust is extremely important as without trust there may be fear. Activities must be enjoyable and suited to the ability of the age group.

10. Only procedures and techniques that are age-appropriate, non-traumatic and respect the rights of children are to be implemented. At no stage should force be used.

Toddlers must be properly supported to prevent the swallowing of water. Techniques such as throwing the toddler into the water from a height and forced back-floating are not recommended. Only when the toddler can demonstrate competent learnt response breath control can submersions be initiated. These submersions should initially be brief and few in number. Once the child can consistently initiate submersions and demonstrate competent breath control submersions can become longer and more frequent. These experiences should be free of force, punishment or threat.

Preschool Stage (42-48 Months)

Preschool children may be capable of learning basic aquatic techniques and participating independently within a class structure. Skill development and water safety education is based on games and activities. It is important that parents understand that the philosophy of programs for this age group is based on water familiarisation as opposed to swimming stroke development.

1. Teachers conducting programs for 42-48 months must be certified and must display an aptitude towards and enthusiasm for teaching this age group.

2. Teachers conducting preschool programs in outdoor facilities may need to adjust class structure and duration in consideration of water and air temperature.

The air temperature and often the water temperature at outdoor venues cannot be controlled. Lessons should be scheduled for the warmest part of the day and should not exceed 30 minutes. Children should be kept active within the water and not left sitting on the edge, where cooler air temperature may cause rapid loss of body heat. The learning of aquatic skills should never take precedence over the child's comfort and welfare.

3. Each infant should be treated as an individual and allowed to progress at her or his own rate.

It is essential that teachers, parents and caregivers understand the needs and fears of preschoolers. They need reassurance and encouragement. Trust is extremely important, as without trust there may be fear and no enjoyment. Activities must be enjoyable and suited to the ability and age of the group.

4. The teacher-pupil ratio should be low to take into account the needs of the students.

Irrespective of aquatic ability, no student should be considered water-safe. Students need to be under adult supervision. A low teacher-pupil ratio of a maximum of 1:5 allows for better supervision and meets the needs of the individual student.

Chapter 2

INFANT HEALTH AND SAFETY

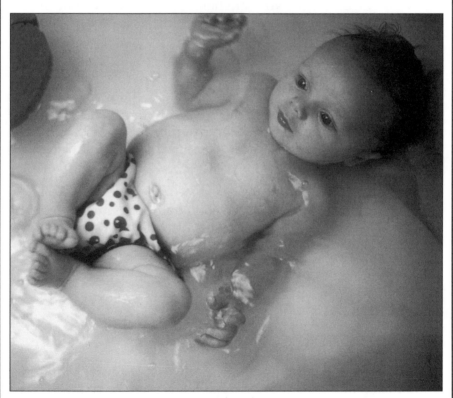

Introduction

Parents may provide their infants and preschool children with aquatic experiences in a range of different environments. These include the bath, home swimming pool and spa, public swimming pool and even the sea. However, when conducting an infant aquatics program, the teacher must ensure that an optimum learning environment is provided and that health and safety issues are addressed, along with issues of programming. Parents may need to be advised about the preparation of their infants and children prior to class and the steps they should take during class to ensure the health and safety of all participants.

While the responsibility of water treatment and disinfection of the pool is the concern of the pool management, there are a number of ways that teachers can help parents to become more aware of the role they play in maintaining a clean, healthy and safe environment.

Environmental Safety

Careful consideration should be given to the environment in which an infant aquatics program is conducted. Several factors relevant to infants require attention. These include the following.

Sun Protection

Where programs are to be conducted in outdoor venues, adequate protection from the sun should be provided for participants. Protection should be in the form of sunscreen, shade cloth, umbrellas or protective clothing.

Teachers and parents also require protection from the sun's damaging rays. A solar suit and a wide-brimmed hat provide suitable protection.

Water Quality

It is important that the water in which the infant aquatics program is conducted meets statutory regulations pertaining to swimming pool water quality. The water should be clear enough that the pool floor can be seen at all depths and should be adequately disinfected. Low levels of disinfectant lead to an increased risk of infection, particularly at higher water temperatures.

Water and Air Temperature

The temperature of the water and air is an important factor in providing an optimum learning environment. The water temperature should ideally be maintained between 30 and 34 degrees Celsius (86 and 93 degrees Fahrenheit). Where the water temperature is less than ideal, consideration should be given to either shortening or cancelling the lesson.

Sun protection is essential for outdoor programs.

Infant aquatic education programs are largely passive. Consequently the loss of body heat is rapid and can have severe repercussions. Parents should be advised to remove their infants from the water if excessive shivering or blueness around the lips, fingers or toes is observed.

Ideally, the air temperature should be maintained at approximately 2 degrees higher than the temperature of the water to ensure participant and teacher comfort.

Pool Surfaces

The floor surfaces in the pool environment, including changing rooms, passageways and pool surrounds, should be slip-resistant and non-abrasive. Ideally the bottom of the pool should also be slip-resistant.

Infant Health and Hygiene

To ensure the maintenance of good health, infant aquatic teachers and parents need to be aware of a number of health and hygiene issues related to participation in aquatic activities. The following factors should be considered.

Sun Exposure

Numerous educational programs emphasise the need for protection from the sun. Despite the programs, many people still ignore the warnings. It is the responsibility of the infant aquatics teacher to educate parents and infants about the dangers associated with sun exposure and about sensible sun exposure and protection. Teach *slip* on a shirt, *slop* on sunscreen and *slap* on a hat, and behave as a positive role model to further convey this important message.

Teachers should model sun-safe practices.

Parents need to be warned that as some sunscreen creams make an infant very slippery and difficult to hold, extra care is required.

It is important to also emphasise that sunburn is not the only danger associated with over-exposure to the sun; dehydration, heat exhaustion and sunstroke may also result and require immediate medical attention.

Hypothermia

Infants and young children lose core body heat quickly if exposed to cold conditions. If the water and air temperature are less than recommended, lessons should be shortened or cancelled.

Symptoms of the onset of hypothermia in infants include

- a blue tinge in the skin and loss of body colour,
- unsettled behaviour and unhappiness,
- lack of interest in the activity, and
- lethargy and tiredness.

Note that very young infants may not shiver when they are cold.

When babies have been chilled through excessive heat loss, they should be given a warm bath or shower until their body temperature rises.

Parents should also be taught how to hold infants to avoid excessive heat loss and should be encouraged to keep the shoulders and torso immersed in the water for as much of the session as possible. Cradling infants against the body and holding them up to the shoulder level, out of the water, exposes them to the chilling effect of the air and accelerates heat loss. A T-shirt may also help to reduce heat loss.

Classes should start on time and infants should not be left waiting around in their bathing suits. Parents should avoid taking infants and children into the pool to play before classes commence.

A warm shower will help warm an infant who is chilled.

Infants need to be warmed, dried and dressed after class. This is especially important during the winter months.

At the conclusion of the lesson parents should dress their infants and children in warm clothing to reduce the risk of hypothermia. Teachers should encourage parents to bring extra towels and warm clothes, including a hat and footwear, and to dry and dress their children as soon as they leave the water to promote rewarming.

Hyponatremia (Water Intoxication)

Hyponatremia may occur if an infant ingests a large volume of water during a short period of time. Ingesting a large volume of water causes dilution of the blood and loss of ions through increased urine output. A change in blood composition will affect brain function, and this may cause lethargy, vomiting, increased urine output, unconsciousness and convulsions.

Cases of water intoxication are very rare. However, forcible or repeated submersions increase the risk. Once children can demonstrate breath control and clear their mouths of water they can be encouraged to make more frequent submersions.

Infant aquatics teachers need to make parents aware of the need to check regularly to ensure that they are holding their infants correctly and that the infants' mouths are clear of the water. Symptoms of water intoxication may not be evident until after the aquatic program. Symptoms include distended stomach, increased irritability and vomiting. Medical advice should be sought immediately.

Airway Protective Reflexes and the Development of Breath Control

Young infants possess an airway protective reflex, which is triggered by receptors around the face and in the larynx (voice box) that cause it to close firmly to prevent fluid entering the lungs. Additionally, the reflex may cause breathing to stop and the heart rate to slow until the airway is re-established. As the infant matures, voluntary control of swallowing develops and the primitive airway protective reflex weakens. This reflex is very sensitive in young infants and can be elicited when air is blown or water is splashed on the face. This reflex should not be relied upon to introduce submersions. Submersions should only occur with infants who display readiness and have sufficient breath control to prepare for submersion and hold their breath for a short time (i.e. 1-4 seconds). Infants who are submerged when they are unprepared will have difficulty in expelling water from their mouths and airways and will tend to swallow it.

Older infants therefore need to be taught to prepare for submersion and to anticipate breath-holding at will. The change from reflexive to voluntary control takes time and typically begins to become established in the Baby 1 stage, at about 6-9 months of age.

The coordination of swimming and breath-holding patterns is established later and is more characteristic of the Toddler 2 stage (36-42 months).

Breath Control Skills Profile

The following profile of breath control skills is a guide only and refers to infants and young children who have had considerable experience in the aquatic program. Newcomers at any stage will need time to learn and adapt their breath-holding skills and will typically perform like younger infants.

- Newborn (birth to 6 months): Reflex breath-holding. Towards the end of this stage infants may begin to cough and choke as the reflexes weaken.
- Baby 1 (6-12 months): May begin to anticipate and prepare for breath-holding through association with cues such as songs and simple commands (e.g. 'one, two, three'). Brief assisted submersions may be possible if signs of readiness are displayed.
- Baby 2 (12-24 months): May begin to initiate own face submersions and will do so in imitation.
- Toddler 1 (24-36 months): May begin to coordinate breath-holding with independent propulsion in water.
- Toddler 2 (36-42 months): May begin to take repeated breaths with independent propulsion in water.
- Preschooler (42-48 months): May be able to coordinate breaths with early swimming action in a rhythmical fashion.

Independent and coordinated breath-holding and breath-taking skills will be determined by a number of factors, particularly water confidence and familiarity with the water through earlier involvement in infant aquatic classes. Differences in temperament and learning styles may cause some infants and children to be naturally more cautious, and they may take considerably longer to build confidence with these skills.

Bowel Motions and Vomiting

All bodily emissions must be viewed as potential sources of infection and care should be taken when working in the aquatic environment to ensure that there is minimal opportunity for transference of infection through this means. Disinfection of the water will, under normal circumstances, destroy infectious agents. However, disinfection requires time and will not be effective when substances pass directly from person to person. Solid matter such as faeces contains many infectious organisms. Escheria coli and cryptosporidium infections are a major concern for aquatic programs involving infants who are not toilet-trained. Contamination of the pool with either vomit or faeces must be regarded as a serious threat to the health of all participants and requires immediate action.

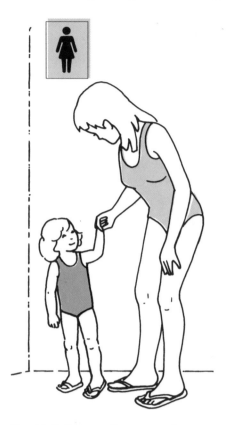

Good toileting practices promote hygienic conditions in the pool.

Many infants are not toilet-trained when they begin an aquatics program and may still be wearing nappies or diapers. Where possible, infants should be encouraged to use the toilet immediately prior to the lesson. During the lesson, snug, fitted lightweight pants that prevent faeces escaping into the pool should be worn. Conventional nappies or diapers should not be worn in the water. Disposable swim pants are now available for use in aquatic environments.

If a bowel motion (or vomiting) occurs during the lesson and matter escapes into the water, all particles of the offending waste must immediately be removed from the water. All participants must evacuate the affected area for approximately 30 minutes, to allow the area to become disinfected. Infants should also be removed immediately from the water when they soil their pants and thoroughly cleaned before they return to the pool in a clean pair of pants.

Medical Considerations and Criteria for Exclusion of Infants and Children Who Are Unwell

A medical form detailing any special conditions should be completed prior to the commencement of classes, and infant and preschool aquatics teachers should be familiar with infants in their class who have special needs. Where parents participate in the program, a medical form should also be completed by them to indicate their own health status.

Exclusion of an infant from an aquatic program is recommended when there is a health risk to other participants. While there are no specific recommendations for exclusion of participants from public swimming pools or aquatic programs, the normal guidelines for exclusion from group settings such as preschool or school programs are applicable.

The following guidelines for exclusion for infants and children in Australia are from *Guidelines for the Control of Infectious Diseases* (published by the Infectious Diseases Unit, Public Health Division, Victorian Department of Human Services).

Disease or condition	Exclusion of cases	Exclusion of contacts
Chickenpox	Until fully recovered or at least one week after the eruption first appears.	Not excluded
Conjunctivitis (acute infectious)	Until discharge from eyes has ceased.	Not excluded
Diphtheria	Until receipt of a medical certificate of recovery from infection.	Domiciliary contacts excluded until investigated by a medical or health officer and shown to be clear of infection.
Giardiasis (diarrhoea)	Until diarrhoea ceases.	Not excluded
Hepatitis A (infectious hepatitis)	Until receipt of a medical certificate of recovery from infection or on subsidence of symptoms.	Not excluded
Hepatitis B	Until recovered from acute attack.	Not excluded
Impetigo (school sores)	Until sores have fully healed. The child may be allowed to return earlier provided that appropriate treatment has commenced and that sores on exposed surfaces such as scalp, face, hands or legs are properly covered with occlusive dressings.	Not excluded

(continued)

(continued)

Disease or condition	Exclusion of cases	Exclusion of contacts
Leprosy	Until receipt of a medical certificate of recovery from infection.	Not excluded
Measles	Until at least 5 days from the appearance of rash or until receipt of a medical certificate of recovery from infection.	Non-immunised contacts must be excluded for 13 days from the first day of appearance of rash in the last case unless immunised within 72 hours of first contact.
Meningococcal infection	Until receipt of a medical certificate of recovery from infection.	Domiciliary contacts must be excluded until they have been receiving appropriate chemotherapy for at least 48 hours.
Mumps	Until fully recovered.	Not excluded
Pediculosis (head lice)	Until appropriate treatment has commenced.	Not excluded
Pertussis (whooping cough)	Until two weeks after the onset of illness and until receipt of a medical certificate of recovery from infection.	Domiciliary contacts must be excluded from attending a children's services centre for 21 days after the last exposure to infection if the contacts have not previously had whooping cough or immunisation against whooping cough.
Poliomyelitis	Until at least 14 days after onset of illness and until receipt of a medical certificate of recovery from infection.	Not excluded
Ringworm	Until appropriate treatment has commenced.	Not excluded
Rotavirus (diarrhoea)	Until diarrhoea ceases.	Not excluded
Rubella	Until fully recovered or at least 5 days after the onset of rash.	Not excluded
Scabies	Until appropriate treatment has commenced.	Not excluded

Disease or condition	Exclusion of cases	Exclusion of contacts
Shigellosis (diarrhoea)	Until diarrhoea ceases.	Not excluded
Streptococcal infection including scarlet fever	Until receipt of a medical certificate of recovery from infection.	Not excluded
Trachoma	Until appropriate treatment has commenced.	Not excluded
Tuberculosis	Until receipt of a medical certificate from a health officer that the child is not considered to be infectious.	Not excluded
Typhoid and paratyphoid fevers	Until receipt of a medical certificate of recovery from infection.	Not excluded unless a medical officer considers exclusion to be necessary.

Parents should be encouraged to avoid bringing infants to class when the infants have a fever or other symptoms such as a rash or runny nose. These symptoms are often the signs of infection, and the affected infants are a risk to other infants in the class. Infants who have any symptoms of diarrhoea or vomiting should be excluded until they are fully recovered. Infants who are unwell will also be at greater risk of hypothermia and will not be able to attend to and gain full benefit from the program. Parents should be helped to understand that infants and preschool children will only benefit from the program when they are healthy and able to actively participate in and enjoy the program.

Skin Conditions

Plantar Warts

These are warts, usually on the soles of the feet. The virus causing these warts spreads within the pool surrounds, including showers and other surfaces. Warts should be treated and the affected areas kept covered until the warts have gone.

Skin Rashes

These may be caused by a sensitivity to chlorinated water or a range of other factors. Medical opinion should be sought to determine the cause. Infants who have rashes and other symptoms such as fever should be excluded from the program and medical opinion sought. Any weeping or open wound should be treated and healed before infants and children resume class. Medical advice may need to be sought for children with eczema.

Eyes

Eye Irritation

Some individuals may have a sensitivity to the chemicals used to treat the water. However, when most participants appear to be affected, eye irritation is a sign of poor water treatment. This should be brought to the attention of the pool management.

Conjunctivitis

Conjunctivitis is a highly contagious eye infection which may be transmitted through the water and via toys and flotation equipment. As noted earlier, affected individuals should be excluded until treated.

Ears

Some infants have grommets (tubes) placed in the ear drum to allow secretions to drain from the middle ear. There is significant debate around whether children with grommets should be allowed to participate in an aquatic program due to the risk of water passing through the grommet and infecting the middle ear. Parents of children with grommets should consult their doctor regarding participation in an aquatic program.

Sniffing

Continuous sniffing as a result of a cold or minor throat infection can result in middle ear infection. Infants and preschool children who sniff are at risk of causing an infection to move from the nasal cavity into the middle ear via the Eustachian tube. Infants and young children should be discouraged from sniffing and encouraged to gently blow their noses before and during the lesson. Tissues and a bin should be provided and parents should be encouraged to attend to and wipe the nose of their own infant to reduce the incidence of cross infection. Older toddlers and preschool children should be encouraged to use tissues and dispose of the tissues immediately.

Resuscitation of Infants and Young Children

Teachers of infant aquatics should hold an approved resuscitation qualification (certification) and update it on an annual basis.

The resuscitation of infants and children is often given minimal consideration in training programs, and rarely do participants have access to infant and child manikins. This is unfortunate, as the majority of the participants in swimming and water safety programs are under 10 years of age.

When resuscitating infants and children the following are to be considered.

Survival Rates

For each infant or child drowning fatality, there are three to four hospital admissions of near-drowned children. Immediate CPR action by trained personnel has assisted many immersion victims to stay alive.

Hypothermia

Full recovery has been reported in child victims totally immersed in ice-cold water for periods of up to one hour. Resuscitation procedures should always begin immediately and continue until an ambulance arrives.

Teachers should regularly practise mouth-to-mouth and mouth-to-nose resuscitation on an infant manikin.

Airway Management

Infants

It can be very difficult to maintain an open airway due to the shortness of the infant's neck and the soft and pliable airway, which is easily distorted by an inappropriate head tilt. The head should be kept in a horizontal position with neither the chin tucked nor the neck extended.

Children

The degree to which the head is tilted varies with the age of the child. The rescuer must be prepared to use jaw support, a very slight head tilt, or jaw thrust until an open airway is achieved. As the child grows, a greater degree of head tilt is required.

In all age groups the lower jaw should be supported, with care taken to avoid pressure on the soft tissues of the neck.

Any foreign object obstructing the airway should be removed by placing the child or infant face down across the rescuer's knees with the head lower than the chest. Back blows or lateral chest thrusts should be used to displace the object.

Infant head position for Expired Air Resuscitation.

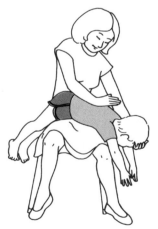

Rescuer delivering back blows to a child supported across the knee in a head-down position.

Preferred Airway

As infants are nasal breathers, it is important to clear the nasal passages. The rescuer should attempt to cover the infant's mouth and nose, but if this is not possible, apply mouth to nose. Mouth to mouth is suitable for children.

Inflation Volume

The volume of expired air required for resuscitation is that sufficient to cause the rise of the lower chest. Infants only require small puffs from the cheeks, while children require a slightly larger volume. Over-inflation may cause distension of the stomach and regurgitation.

Breathing and Expired Air Resuscitation Rates

Age	Rate
Infant: birth to 1 year	20 puffs per minute (1 every 3 seconds)
Child: 1-8 years	20 small breaths per minute (1 every 3 seconds)

Pulse Check

An infant has a relatively short neck, which makes the carotid artery difficult to locate. The pulse provided by the brachial artery on the inside of the upper arm is easier to locate. For children, the carotid artery provides a suitable pulse. The normal pulse rate for an infant or child is 100 beats per minute (i.e. approximately 15 beats in 10 seconds).

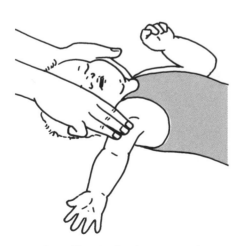

Location of brachial pulse on an infant.

Compression Point and Technique

The compression point is identified by locating the lower extremity of the sternum and applying compression above this point. For infants, the tips of two fingers should be placed immediately above this point. For children, place the heel of one hand above the point. The compression depth and rates must be adjusted to the size of the infant or child.

The hand or fingers must not extend below the lower end of the sternum.

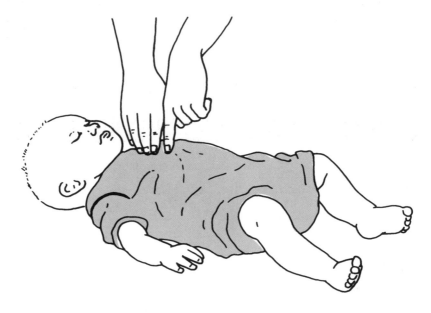

Location of compression point for CPR on child and infant.

Infant and child CPR rates	
One-operator CPR	Two breaths and 15 compressions in 10 seconds
Two-operator CPR	One breath and 5 compressions in 3 seconds

Compression Depth

Infant	1 cm (1/3 in.) approximately
Child	1–2 cm (1/3–3/4 in.)

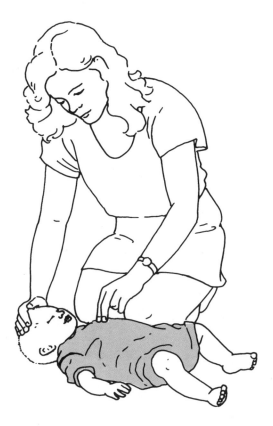

Infant compression technique, using two fingers.

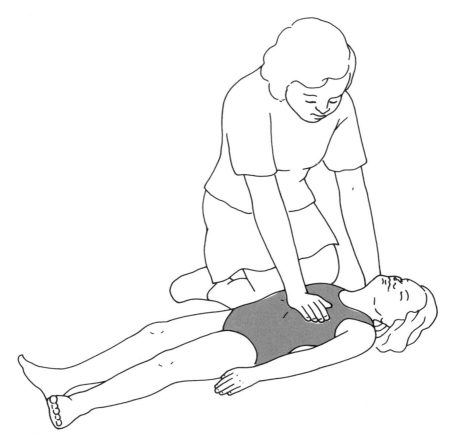

Child compression technique, using heel of one hand.

Transportation

If the child is small enough to be carried, this is often the preferred method of transportation. Care should be taken to ensure that the child maintains a body temperature as close to normal as the circumstances allow.

Chapter 3

DEVELOPMENT

Introduction

Infant aquatics teachers require an understanding of the major developmental characteristics of infants and young children. This understanding will enable teachers to appreciate the implications for aquatic education as children move through key developmental stages. As new motor, cognitive, communication and personal competencies develop, infants' and young children's readiness for learning new skills will change.

Motor Development

The development of movement occurs through an orderly process that moves from a period of reflex control during early infancy towards a process of voluntary control. As the early infantile reflexes weaken and disappear, infants learn to master new patterns of movement. With practice, infants learn to initiate, time and sequence these patterns into organised voluntary movements. As shown in the box, skilled movements are built up over time as infants learn to adapt and organise new motor patterns. Controlled, organised swimming takes many years to occur.

Reflex control

↓

Reflexes weaken and disappear (a period of transitional movements)

↓

New motor patterns emerge (immature and voluntary control)

↓

Skilled control established as patterns are integrated through practice

These changes can be seen in the progressive stages of aquatic skill development. For example:

Reflex swimming (0–3 months)

Disorganised responses (3–9 months)

Emergent patterns for breath control, head control, buoyancy, arm stroke, leg kick (6 months to 4 years)

Gradual integration of underlying patterns leading to coordinated swimming movements (3–7 years)

In the case of aquatic skills, as with all motor skills, infants' responses are initially reflexive and are not able to be regulated. As the early reflexes weaken, infants become less organised and struggle to adapt their movements to their environment. During this transitional period infants roll from front to back and flounder due to disorganised movements of their limbs, which stem from problems of buoyancy and balance.

Infants will also have problems with controlling their breathing and often cough and swallow water. It is important during this time that they are given adequate physical support in the water. They are then able to play and splash the water and begin to engage in their own learning about the aquatic environment. They begin to establish a more organised and voluntary response to it. This organisation requires infants to learn how to coordinate the movements associated with buoyancy, head and breath control and basic stroke and kicking patterns before they begin to learn more formal swimming, as illustrated here.

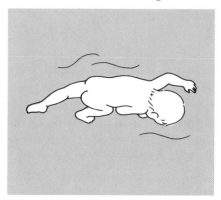

Infants display automatic or reflex 'swimming-type' movements when they are placed face down in the water.

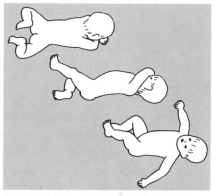

During the transitional period infants are unstable in the water and will roll and flounder.

Toddlers and preschoolers are beginning to show more organised responses, and preschoolers show good adaptation to the water.

The development of aquatic skills parallels the development of land-based skills that normally occurs during the first three to four years of life as infants and children learn to walk, run, jump and hop. These land-based movements emerge as patterns for posture, balance and locomotion become integrated. Daily experiences derived from the demands of moving provide infants and children with essential feedback for coordinating movements into smoothly sequenced actions. In the same way, infants and toddlers who are introduced to aquatic experiences early in life will have the opportunity to learn about the many different aspects of being in an aquatic environment. By the age of four years many experienced preschoolers have mastered the basic elements of swimming and are ready to develop a skilled swimming style.

> Readiness for each stage of swimming will be determined by both the maturity of the child and previous aquatic experiences. Readiness refers to what infants can do, not just their age. For instance, infants who are relaxed and able to float on their backs with little support will be ready to move on to a more advanced float with less or no support. Infants who voluntarily submerge their faces for short periods are ready to learn to do repeated breath-holding.

An understanding of the motor development of infants and preschool children helps to explain many of their characteristics in an aquatic environment. In the following sections the development of aquatic skills is contrasted with the development of land-based skills. This demonstrates that aquatic skills progress as naturally as land-based movements when infants and young children are given regular experiences in water.

Newborn Stage (Birth to 6 Months)

Characteristics

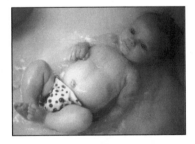

- Movement is regulated by as many as 70 different neonatal reflexes.
- Movement is also characterised by spontaneous kicking and general activity.
- Neonatal reflexes begin to weaken or become inhibited within the first three months of life.
- New patterns for posture and locomotion begin to emerge, making voluntary responses possible.

Reflexes regulate the infant's response to stimuli such as touch and body position and to the aquatic environment. Some reflexes are essential for survival and regulate responses necessary for control over breathing and feeding. Other reflexes provide early organisation of movement responses necessary for posture, patterns of locomotion, manipulation and an early response to being startled. Some examples of these neonatal reflexes are listed in the following table.

Reflex	Stimuli	Response	Developmental course for this reflex
Postural			
Head righting	Supporting infant in an upright posture.	Head held upright momentarily.	Improves with age. Leads to head control as in sitting/standing etc.
Asymmetric tonic neck reflex (sometimes referred to as the *fencing position*)	Infant is placed prone with head turned to one side.	Limbs on the side of the body to which the face is pointing are extended while the limbs on the opposite side of the body are flexed.	Normally weakens and disappears.
Locomotion			
Stepping	Infant supported upright with feet touching surface.	Infant steps using a whole foot pattern.	Weakens and disappears in most infants. Re-emerges prior to voluntary stepping.
Crawling	Infant placed face down and pressure applied alternately to each foot.	Coordinated creeping movements of the arms and legs.	Weakens and disappears and replaced with voluntary crawling.
Swimming	Infant held horizontal above a surface or in water.	Coordinated movements of legs and arms with sideward bending of the trunk.	Disappears and replaced with voluntary swimming.

(continued)

(continued)

Reflex	Stimuli	Response	Developmental course for this reflex
Moro reflex	Infant is startled, e.g. by a loud noise.	Limbs extend away from the body and then flex back onto the body. The infant usually cries.	Disappears and replaced with startle response.
Manipulation			
Palmar grasp	A soft touch is applied to the palm of the hand.	Fingers flex and grasp.	Disappears and replaced with voluntary grasping.
Breathing			
Airway protective response	Sensitive to a wide range of stimuli, e.g. blowing/ splashing water on the face or submerging the face in water.	Larynx closes to block entrance to airways. Also active during feeding to assist swallowing.	Reflex becomes more regulated and is elicited by more specific stimuli and integrated with mechanisms for speech.

The reflexes disappear and weaken before organised skills emerge. Typically these early reflexes have weakened considerably by 3 months of age and have usually disappeared by 6-9 months. The period 4-9 months is a transitional stage of motor behaviour in which infants progress from reflex to voluntary movement. The effects of this transition are evident in the aquatic environment, and while the swimming reflex makes infants appear highly organised in the water, this period is soon followed by a time in which infants are disorganised and struggle to adapt to the water. Goal-directed movement re-emerges and by about 10 months of age the infant may display much greater adaptation to the water.

Postural and motor development are also characterised by two trends referred to as the *cephalocaudal* and *proximodistal* patterns. The cephalocaudal pattern describes the sequence of postural control that begins first with control over the upper body and then a gradual shift towards the lower body (*cephalo* = head, *caudal* = foot). Thus postural control of the head and neck precedes postural control of the torso and hips. For this reason infants require initial support for their head position, while at later stages this support can shift down towards the torso and hips.

The proximodistal pattern refers to the sequence where control is established towards the centre of the body and then gradually moves out towards the limbs (*proximo* = near and *distal* = far). Thus infants master weight-bearing through their shoulders and hips prior to weight-bearing through elbows and knees etc. In water, infants establish balance of their bodies before being able to coordinate arms and legs for propulsion.

Major Motor Milestones

Age	Aquatic environment	On 'land'
Neonate	Swimming reflex. Airway protective response requires assistance with head control. Buoyant body, floats on back with assistance.	Neonatal reflexes. Random writhing and kicking. Minimal head control.
12 weeks +	Swimming reflex weakening. Able to float on back but may try to lift head, resulting in more instability. Prone position can be encouraged with support.	Neonatal reflexes weakening. Lifts heads and takes weight on elbows when placed in prone position. Supports head when held sitting or in the upright position.
16–24 weeks	Swimming reflex continues to weaken and will have disappeared in some infants. Some infants 'swim' under water with self-direction. Rolling movements and head-raising movements increase infants' instability in the water.	Rolls from stomach to back and later from back to stomach. Begins to sit with support. Creeps along with stomach in contact with floor.

Implications for Teaching and Learning

Very young infants require support and guidance in water and they should not be expected to rely on their neonatal reflex for swimming. Teachers need to remember that this is an involuntary pattern and cannot be regulated or adapted by young infants. Infants' responses to the aquatic environment are also hampered because they are unable to lift and turn their heads for breathing. The airway protective response will further hamper infants' breathing, as they are also unable to moderate this response and the airways will automatically be closed off when these stimuli to the face and mouth are present. Infants in this age group may be placed at risk when there are inappropriate practices involving submersion.

The airway protective response must also become regulated by voluntary mechanisms before infants can integrate this pattern in a controlled manner. The development of breath control follows the same course of development shown by many other reflexes. Reflex control at birth becomes integrated with voluntary movements for speech and breath-holding. Before infants can stay under the water for any length of time they must be able to block the normal reflex to take a breath. To release a breath while the face is submerged requires the ability to relax this reflex even though the face is submerged.

Infants require considerable postural support to experience the water in an organised manner. They can be cradled and moved gently through the water to feel the sensation of moving in an aquatic environment. Infants have good buoyancy due to their body fat and, provided they are given adequate support through the head and shoulders, they can be assisted to float on their backs and stomachs, although care must be taken to ensure their faces are kept free of the water. These early experiences can be conducted in the bathtub at home or in a suitably warmed swimming pool.

As infants gain postural control over the head and shoulder region and start to reach out towards objects, they may enjoy supported activities on their stomachs as well as their backs. Again, these experiences may be conducted in a very shallow bath or in a pool environment with support or using flotation aids.

At approximately 4 months of age infants may appear less stable as they attempt to raise the head and begin to roll in preparation for a sitting position. In the aquatic environment good support is required during this phase of development. Supervision is especially important during activities on flotation mats to prevent an infant from rolling into the water.

Baby 1 Stage (6-12 Months)

Characteristics

• This phase is one of preparation for walking. The major motor tasks for infants are to master voluntary control over their posture, locomotion movements and manipulative skills. Infants master posture in the upright position, for sitting and standing, and then begin to move voluntarily from one position to another.

• Infants learn to control their locomotion as they master the ability to roll from front to back and from back to front, crawl, pull themselves up into standing and begin to walk independently.

• Manipulative skills also become more controlled during this phase as infants master the ability to pick objects up using a fine grasp between the thumb and forefinger. They also master the ability to let go of objects held in the hand.

• In the aquatic environment infants may begin to master their ability to hold their breath and prepare for submersion as well as splash and kick. They initially require considerable support, but towards the end of this period are beginning to show independence and can propel themselves for short distances such as between parent and teacher.

The major postural and motor achievements during this period are listed here.

Major Motor Milestones

Age	Aquatic environment	On 'land'
Posture and locomotion		
5–8 months	Needs support of the trunk. Has good head control. Is unstable and rolls easily.	Sits with support.
8 months	Likes to be upright and may dislike being on the back.	Sits without support, crawls. Stepping begins to emerge.
10 months	When supported uses arm and leg movements for propulsion.	Sits independently, maintains and recovers balance. Stands holding onto furniture.
10–15 months	May begin to propel self around when given adequate support.	Maintains an upright position. Establishes walking: walks 'holding on' then walks independently.
Manipulation		
6–12 months	Enjoys games with toys, will fetch, collect and drop them into small buckets.	Refines grasping and releasing. By 12 months can reach, grasp and release objects at will.
Breath control		
6–9 months	May begin to voluntarily initiate breath-holding and may do so in response to cues such as 'ready, set, go' or 'one, two, three'.	Babbles, makes bubbles and spits food.
9–12 months	Some can anticipate and hold their breath for submersion for short periods.	Will blow bubbles. Imitates sounds.

Implications for Teaching and Learning

Infants assume a more upright posture in the aquatic environment. They require a lot of encouragement for floating or moving on their backs. This can be facilitated through eye contact with a familiar caregiver. Rolling over will be more easily initiated, and this makes them less stable in water, particularly when they look up and turn their heads. They will enjoy sitting and being placed on their stomachs on flotation mats. As infants gain greater postural control and kick more vigorously, they enjoy moving around with lighter support.

Activities should be conducted with support at chest level and later at the hips. Infants should not be forced to be on their backs beyond their level of willingness. Care should be taken to ensure the mouth and face are kept clear of the water. Towards the latter part of this stage infants may be able to anticipate some sequences and may begin to learn simple cues in order to prepare for submersion. These experiences should be positive for infants. Only when an infant displays full anticipation and readiness should brief periods of submersion be initiated.

A range of interesting activities can be offered with toys for infants to grasp at and to drop into an open bucket. Soft squeeze toys will be easier for younger infants to clutch.

Infants in the Baby 1 stage will enjoy opportunities to explore the water independently.

Infants will be more motivated to explore when there are toys for play.

Baby 2 Stage (12-24 Months)

Characteristics

- Walking becomes automatic so that by the end of the second year infants walk with ease and stop and start walking without difficulty. Running also appears around this time.

- Their independence and drive to explore put these infants at risk. Statistics show that this age group has the highest incidence of drowning.

- Manoeuvrability improves as the feet come closer together and the infant is able to move around objects and corners. Infants are still top-heavy due to the proportionately larger head and shorter legs.

- In the water infants may begin to show improved coordination as their posture becomes more horizontal. Many are able to use their arms and legs to propel themselves around with the assistance of a flotation aid.

- They are more able to cope with water in their mouths and spit it out when necessary. Submersion may become more acceptable. Many may begin to bob under the water independently as this period progresses. Controlled rhythmic breathing may appear.

Major Motor Milestones

Age	Aquatic environment	On 'land'
12 months +	Upright posture. May propel self using a flotation aid. Arms are relatively close to the body and may be used in an early breaststroke action. Legs move with pump action. Rolling is organised and controlled.	Walks independently. Feet are wide apart and flat-footed, knees are bent and the body leans. Arms are used to assist balance.
18 months	Posture becomes more horizontal. Arms are used more effectively to pull the body. Legs may show a number of patterns and may be relatively straight or used in a cycling motion.	Walks with speed, but does not run. Feet are still apart and the knees bent. Arms move in towards the body.
24 months	Posture horizontal. Arms are extended more and pull more effectively. Legs are straight and kicking is more effective. Breath control may be well established and may be integrated with a whole pattern of early swimming-type movement and bobbing down under the water.	Walking is still immature, the feet are closer together and the posture is more upright. Running is immature, with feet apart and arms out for balance.

Implications for Teaching and Learning

Infants enjoy a wide variety of aquatic experiences and are beginning to explore more independence. Their early explorations are typically in a more vertical position and they use their legs in a pump action, similar to their flat-footed walking pattern, to propel themselves around. As they may begin to assume a more horizontal position in the water, they begin to use the arms more actively to pull themselves along and the legs may be used in a pump action. Support through flotation aids may be gradually reduced throughout this stage. Some infants will be able to propel themselves along with sufficient head control to support breathing.

Infants in this age group are able to prepare to hold their breath when submerging and should be able to learn to successfully expel water from their mouths. With experience, they can begin to bring the head up in the mid-line to take a breath when they are paddling through the water.

Increased mobility and independence will permit infants to engage in a range of activities such as paddling short distances from teacher to parent or to paddle short distances from a flotation mat to a parent and to experiment with a number of ways of entering the water.

Toddler 1 Stage (24-36 Months)

Characteristics

- Balance improves, strength increases and movements are more smoothly coordinated.

- Walking and running patterns improve as the toddler gains a more upright posture, the feet come closer together and the arms and legs begin to swing in opposition.

- Improved strength enables toddlers to lift their weight for jumping and later hopping.

- By the third birthday toddlers can balance on a preferred foot and stand on tiptoes.

- In the aquatic environment toddlers are working towards further coordination of breath control, buoyancy, arm and leg movements and, by the end of this stage, the swimming pattern may be developing into a beginner's stroke.

Major Motor Milestones

Age	Aquatic environment	On 'land'
24 months	Horizontal body position. Longer push and pull with arms and legs, although not yet fully extended. Repeated breath-holding. Overall pattern may look like early swimming.	Jumping emerges. The early pattern is immature with uneven use of the feet for propelling the body. Little use of the arms or bending of the knees for take-off.
36 months	May be more of a shift towards a rudimentary crawl.	Jumps with two feet together. Walks well. Balances on a preferred foot and stands on tiptoe. May be able to hop one or two hops on the preferred foot.

Implications for Teaching and Learning

Toddlers who have already had considerable aquatic experiences may show greater confidence in the water and will probably be able to propel themselves for short distances in the water using a beginner's stroke. It is important that toddlers be able to reach the bottom of the pool with their feet. Use of floating platforms and elevated platforms in deeper pools will reassure toddlers, and they will have greater motivation to try out independent manoeuvres in the water. With confidence and improved breath control experienced toddlers may be able to move through the water and may submerge and swim towards the bottom to retrieve toys and objects.

The emergence of jumping will enable toddlers to begin to explore a variety of entries. Towards the third birthday, as toddlers show greater ability to coordinate whole-body movements, safe diving skills may be introduced.

Toddlers who are being introduced to an aquatic program for the first time will not have the same knowledge of the aquatic environment as their peers with more experience. It is important to treat each toddler as an individual and for teachers to take their cues from the level of ability and competence the child demonstrates. Some toddlers may require considerable support from their parents as they learn to adjust to the aquatic environment. They will need time to develop a sense of buoyancy, learn to submerge with confidence and propel themselves before they will be willing to pursue tasks independently. These toddlers will also need some time to learn to judge where the bottom of the pool is.

Many toddlers will be quite fearful in their early aquatic experiences and will benefit best from experiences that allow them to rely on their parents and to gradually build up knowledge of the pool environment and the skills needed for them to become independently mobile in water.

Toddler 2 Stage (36-42 Months)

Characteristics

- The most marked development in this age group is greater coordination of the whole body in large motor skills. The toddler begins to walk more maturely with articulation of the foot and an arm swing. Similarly, running and jumping show improved total integration of the whole body.

- By the age of four years the pattern of walking approximates that of the adult and is smooth and rhythmical.

- In the aquatic environment improved coordination may lead to the development of a rudimentary crawl using a long push-pull arm paddle and a bent-knee kick.

Major Motor Milestones

Age	Aquatic environment	On 'land'
36–42 months	Rudimentary crawl with repeated breath control.	Walks with feet closer together and can walk along a line. Balances on tiptoe and can balance on a preferred foot momentarily. Hops 1 or 2 hops on preferred foot. Jumps with two-foot take-off. Gallops.

Implications for Teaching and Learning

Following the third birthday toddlers show greater coordination of movements through improved organisation and control of the body as a whole. Toddlers with early aquatic experiences will have had more opportunities to develop a range of fundamental water skills, including breath-holding, floating and propulsion using both the arms and legs, and may begin to show an early overarm stroke pattern.

Toddlers in this age range can be expected to demonstrate a wide range of abilities. Individual differences will be determined by a number of factors, including differences in their rates of development and their knowledge and experience of the aquatic environment. Assessment of toddlers' aquatic readiness should include observation of their ability to hold their breath and to expel water from their mouths, their buoyancy and body position and the patterns of arm and leg movements they use for propulsion through the water. This will help establish each toddler's level of competence and confidence in water for appropriate program planning.

Preschool Stage (42-48 Months)

Characteristics

• Preschoolers become taller due to greater growth in their legs. This lowers their centre of gravity and improves their stability on land. Walking, running, jumping and other movements continue to become steadier and more rhythmical, and take on more mature characteristics.

• In the water experienced preschoolers show a more horizontal body position and the arms and legs are more extended and demonstrate an early flutter kick and overarm action. Early swimming using rudimentary flutter kick and overarm action may be evident.

Major Motor Milestones

Age	Aquatic environment	On 'land'
42–48 months	Horizontal body, extended arms and legs. Flutter kicking and overarm action may begin. Jumps into pool and may begin diving.	Walks with a mature gait. Running and jumping show more coordination. May begin to skip.

Implications for Teaching and Learning

Preschoolers need challenges that allow them to extend their physical skills. It is important to continue to structure their environment so they can master skills through play and exploration with others. Children need opportunities to build confidence in the water. While it may be tempting to begin formal stroke training, this should be avoided. Preschoolers' immature stroke and kicking patterns will become more integrated with body position and breath control as the program challenges them to extend their skills through exploration of the water.

Cognitive Development and Communication

Cognitive development is the mental development of the infant and young child. It involves the development of skills associated with thinking and learning and includes the ability to attend to relevant details, to classify and remember, to imagine and develop concepts, to develop strategies necessary for solving problems and to acquire language.

The preschool years are remarkable for the changes that occur in children's understanding about their world. Infants and toddlers grow in their understandings as they begin to attend to new stimuli from events and objects and have the opportunity to socialise and explore in a playful manner. Repetition of experiences will enable infants and toddlers to develop a mental framework for classifying events and situations. Each new experience will be compared with earlier experiences and then classified by established criteria. There will be times when new experiences cannot be simply assimilated into existing frameworks and new criteria will need to be established in order to more accurately classify new information. In this way mental growth occurs as infants and toddlers reorganise their frameworks for thinking to accommodate new information.

Infants and toddlers take an active role in learning: They are naturally curious and will actively explore cause and effect relationships. This learning is also highly dependent on interaction with their parents and other supportive adults. Parents encourage infant learning when they are sensitive to the infant's cues and when they assist him or her to master each new stage with encouragement and praise.

Parents employ three important strategies that promote learning:

• Strategic support through scaffolding. Parents promote infant learning by being sensitive to what they can do with assistance. Scaffolding involves a teaching-learning relationship in which parents act as experts and provide assistance as it is needed. The skilful parent gradually withdraws this support as the child's own competence emerges.

• Positive guidance through valuing what the infant does and showing recognition of this with encouragement and praise.

• Modelling and demonstrating the desired behaviour. Infants are more likely to imitate the actions of their parents.

Newborn Stage (Birth to 6 Months)

During the first 4 months infants use the reflex patterns they are born with to explore their world. At 4 months they are able to develop more elaborate actions and they begin to explore their world by producing interesting effects of their own on objects. Actions that produce pleasure tend to be repeated. An infant less than 4 months old may splash her or his hand in the water accidentally. However, by about 4 months, the infant will observe the effect of the hand hitting the water and may make deliberate attempts to splash. The infant may giggle and laugh at the consequence of this action.

Very young infants have only a limited memory capacity, as judged by their ability to look for objects that fall from view or are hidden from them. Typically infants aged less than one month show no awareness when an object is moved out of sight. They make no attempt to look at where it was. By about 4 months of age infants may look at where the object was last. This helps explain why infants are easily distracted by new stimuli and will change their attention rapidly.

Infants vocalise during this stage and begin to engage in vocal conversations. By 4 to 6 months they are becoming sensitive to the tone of vocal expression and are sensitive to facial expression. The reactions of their parents play an important role in shaping their responses to new experiences, as infants often look to their parents for a response.

Implications for Teaching and Learning

Infants take an active role in communication and use sustained eye contact and vocalisations such as cooing noises to engage parents in vocal 'conversations'. Their ability to appreciate the nature of the aquatic environment is limited to a sensory motor experience through which they make their own attempts to explore the water in a playful and repetitive manner. They are able to show their enjoyment of these actions, and acceptance and enjoyment of new experiences will be influenced by interactions with their parents. Parents who look at and talk to their infants provide additional emotional support for their children.

Baby 1 Stage (6-12 Months)

From 4 to 8 months infants become more interested in external events and objects, and begin to learn that the environment is responsive to them. Towards 6 months infants understand that actions produce reactions and they expect to see a reaction to their actions. Typically they will repeat a behaviour to repeat an interesting effect. This improved understanding of the relationship between cause and effect leads infants towards goal-directed behaviour. Rewarding events will lead them to explore more action-reaction related events and this will lead further towards extending their mental framework and experimenting to achieve a desired outcome.

Infants in this age group are developing better memories and will begin to look for things that are out of view. For example, if a toy falls and is still partially within view, the infant will strain to see it better. They love to play games such as peek-a-boo, in which people appear and disappear, as they are able to anticipate the return of the player.

Imitation provides an early and effective strategy for learning, and infants in this age group are beginning to imitate both the sounds and actions of others. These achievements are important milestones in learning as infants model their behaviour through interactions with significant people in their lives. Communication skills are also improving as infants begin to imitate speech sounds and work towards producing their first word.

Implications for Teaching and Learning

From about 6 to 8 months of age infants are able to remember and imitate actions, and they also begin to develop and explore their own goals. Their interest in the aquatic environment will be motivated by the desire to explore its properties. Infants will also begin to imitate the behaviours of others in the water. They will be motivated to engage in simple games and may be able to anticipate simple events such as submerging their faces in the water. They will pick up positive and negative cues associated with these events. Enjoyment of the water will be greatly influenced by the opportunities infants have for play and exploration and the interaction between the infant and parent. Simple songs and rhymes begin to provide useful cues for particular activities.

Baby 2 Stage (12-24 Months)

From 12 to 18 months infants' understanding of cause and effect improves, and they begin to use trial and error to solve problems. They are often characterised as being 'true or natural scientists' as they explore the effects of their actions in the environment. The drive to explore events through trial-and-error experimentation means they are often seen to be mischievous; they experiment freely with anything that interests them and is within reach. At home they may pull the toilet paper completely off the roll or drop things in the bowl to see them float or attempt to see if the cat can swim. At the poolside they may throw tissues and other objects in to explore their qualities in the water. This desire to explore is not matched in any way with an appreciation of danger.

The drive to explore at this stage must be fully appreciated by adults. While teachers may encourage enjoyment and learning in an aquatic environment, they cannot afford to make any assumptions about infants' ability to be safe in the water. Goals for and expectations of aquatic programs must be developed within realistic parameters. Happy and secure children may be competent, but this does not mean they are safe. Infants and toddlers must be closely supervised at all times, particularly when they are near swimming pools or other waterways.

Children's explorations, coupled with an improved memory, lead to greater knowledge about each behaviour and its outcome. Children's understanding of the world is enlarged, and they become more aware of events and their outcomes.

Language skills begin to emerge rapidly. The ability to understand what is being said is more developed during this stage than the ability to speak. Songs and rhymes play an important role in helping infants in this stage to listen, rehearse the sounds of speech and attend to simple routines.

Implications for Teaching and Learning

Infants at this stage need opportunities to play and explore in the aquatic environment with greater independence. The aquatic environment should be designed to provide stimulating experiences and should be based around a sense of fun and enjoyment. It should also help to develop a sense of security. Parents should be engaged as both interactive play partners and role models. Parents need to be made aware of how inquisitive infants require constant supervision.

Toddler 1 and 2 Stages (24-42 Months)

At this stage language is still emerging. Toddlers are beginning to express and share ideas verbally. However, their thinking skills are still limited by their ability to make connections between events. This means they are not able to take in the 'big picture' when engaged in any experience. Their thinking is limited by three main characteristics that are clearly related:

- **Centration:** a tendency to focus on only one aspect of an event and ignore all others. This is evident in situations that require problem-solving, such as selecting the biggest object. A toddler will focus on one aspect of the object, say its width, and neglect its other dimensions, such as its thickness. This will prevent the toddler from solving problems flexibly.
- **Egocentrism:** where the significance of any experience is understood through reference to oneself. Toddlers are unable to separate their own experiences from the experiences of others. For example, toddlers will assume that others see what they see and feel what they feel. For this reason a crying toddler may cause other children to feel upset and apprehensive.
- **Concreteness:** where the focus of attention is on the observable characteristics of an event. Toddlers will infer cause and effect directly from what they have observed.

These characteristics mean that toddlers are limited in their understanding of the points of view held by others. They will also attend to the more tangible aspects of an event rather than abstract ideas.

Implications for Teaching and Learning

In learning situations toddlers need to actively participate in experiences rather than be given long explanations and demonstrations by others. Sharing and waiting to take turns will be difficult. Class strategies and strategies for using equipment should ensure that all children can participate at the same time.

Preschool Stage (42-48 Months)

Language and cognition are developing rapidly and preschoolers are very curious about events and their causes. Preschoolers still interpret things literally. They ask a lot of questions but have difficulty in answering questions asked of them. Their language is becoming more grammatical, although they tend to overgeneralise rules of speech, particularly verbs and pronouns. Statements such as 'Her and me are swimming' or 'He don't listen' are not uncommon.

Implications for Teaching and Learning

Preschoolers love to engage in conversations but are somewhat literal in their understanding. They need help to understand cause and effect and need simple explanations. They are helped in making decisions when given simple options.

Personal Development

Infants display a range of emotions that help express their needs and feelings as well as help establish social relationships.

Simple emotions like happiness and anger appear within the first months of life, while the more complex emotions of self-pride, shame and guilt do not appear until the second year of life.

Social relationships initially focus on the primary caregiver and significant others. These early relationships are designed to ensure that these significant caregivers stay close by at all times. Infants are initially completely dependent on their parents. Before infants can be independent they must learn how to discriminate strangers from familiars and how to socially interact with others. Complex social interactions require that infants be able to understand the responses of others to them.

Temperament and personality characteristics account for individual differences in the responses of babies and toddlers. Infants and toddlers demonstrate three main temperament types:

- **The Easy Child:** These infants and children are characterised by their generally happy disposition, and they adjust well to new experiences.
- **The Slow-to-Warm-Up Child:** These infants and children display an initial withdrawal response to new situations and need time to 'warm up' or adjust.
- **The Difficult Child:** These infants and children tend to cry a lot and demonstrate more negative reactions. They have difficulty in adjusting to new situations.

Newborn Stage (Birth to 6 Months)

In the early stages infants are well attuned to the primary caregiver and react more positively to the voice and appearance of this person. However, they are relatively indiscriminate when it comes to others and they will smile at most people. By 3 to 6 months they are becoming more aware of strange situations and show more selective responses to familiar people. By 5 months they can distinguish strangers from family members. At this age they can also display excitement, and they will laugh or vocalise harshly to show their pleasure and displeasure.

Implications for Teaching and Learning

Infants are more responsive to the primary caregiver and more easily calmed by this person. A basic sense of trust in their primary caregiver helps infants establish confidence in their environment. The mood and disposition that parents display to their infant will influence the quality of the infant's sense of trust in the environment.

Infant temperamental characteristics need to be considered. Infants who are difficult or slow to warm up will need more encouragement and a longer time to adapt to the aquatic environment.

Baby 1 Stage (6-12 Months)

Infants demonstrate a wider variety of emotional responses and are actively engaged in interacting socially with others who are familiar to them. They are very sensitive to facial expression and voice tone.

Infants demonstrate definite likes and dislikes, and they will begin to show anxiety at separation from their parent. They will also show fearfulness of strange situations and demonstrate more clingy behaviours towards their primary caregiver.

Implications for Teaching and Learning

Infants are more responsive to their parents and will be more easily introduced to new experiences when parents are actively involved. Infants may protest when handed to a teacher or when the teacher comes too close. It is important to make sure infants' feelings are respected so that they can feel secure when faced with new situations and people. Temperamental characteristics continue to be a factor in adjustment, and some infants will adapt more quickly to strangers than others.

Baby 2 Stage (12-24 Months)

Infants are beginning to show a wider range of emotional responses. They will display jealousy and affection along with anger and fear. They may begin to demonstrate temper tantrums. These changes are important for infants to establish a sense of autonomy in their world. These behaviours become more evident around 18 months of age and are associated with less dependence on the primary caregiver, along with the development of their own self-awareness. Infants will now spend more time away from their parents as they begin to explore their environment on their own. A sense of 'I am' and 'I can' is becoming evident.

Implications for Teaching and Learning

Infants need opportunities to explore for themselves within safe parameters. The environment should provide them with opportunities to explore independently and with safety. In the aquatic environment there should be opportunities for them to practise and explore their aquatic skills with more independence. However, parents must be ready to provide support and to set limitations when needed. Infants in this age group will need guidance in their interactions with others as they learn appropriate ways of interacting.

Toddler 1 and 2 Stages (24-42 Months)

Toddlers are more self-assured. They show greater independence from their primary caregivers and will separate more easily from them. They are also beginning to show greater awareness of routines and simple rules and they are happy to please. Toddlers will help to put things away and are beginning to develop some self-help skills such as dressing with simple clothing and indicating their own toilet needs. They are able to interact in more meaningful ways with their peers and can engage in simple play with them. By the age of 3 years self-control is becoming evident and toddlers are more aware of acceptable social behaviours, although they will need guidance through the use of secure limitations and expectations for behaviour.

Implications for Teaching and Learning

Toddlers are more self-aware and have greater self-control, although they still need positive guidance towards socially acceptable behaviours. Simple rules should be established and compliance should be positively and warmly encouraged in order to assist the development of self-regulation. Classes should be friendly and enjoyable and achievements celebrated. Toddlers in these age groups who get consistent attention by doing what is expected of them will be more cooperative and goal-directed in class.

Preschool Stage (42-48 Months)

Preschoolers are beginning to negotiate friendships. It is not unusual to see 4-year-olds seek out their special friends. Preschoolers are usually able to separate from their parents without a fuss. They have more skills for resolving conflicts and are more able to communicate their ideas. Their limited reasoning and the difficulties they have in taking the perspectives of others may lead to abrupt breakdowns in this communication. Group activities often end with hitting, arguing, insulting and refusing to share. Adults are still needed to assist these negotiations. Adults who firmly reject aggressive behaviour and show children how to help each other, cooperate and show empathy assist preschoolers to find alternative solutions to conflict.

Implications for Teaching and Learning

Preschoolers need warm, caring adults who can set limits firmly and calmly. They enjoy group participation and acceptance by others. Group activities need to be guided by adults who reject aggression and redirect activities.

Small-group settings help children to develop social skills.

AU**S**TSWIM.

Chapter 4

PRINCIPLES OF TEACHER, PARENT AND CHILD RELATIONSHIPS

Introduction

The teacher of an infant aquatic program must appreciate that her or his role involves several areas at the same time: The teacher is involved directly with the infants and children and is also teaching them indirectly through interactions with their parents. The teacher is also interacting with parents and coordinating group activities  involving both parents and infants or children. The interactions that occur require a high level of communication. It is important that the teacher be able to give clear messages that demonstrate sensitivity to all involved. Communications need to be clear and well developed so that they are effective with individual children, individual parents, each child-parent pair and the group of parents and children.

The communication strategies adopted for the class should be designed to

- promote positive feelings in children,
- help the children develop a sense of trust in the environment,
- help children develop a sense of their own autonomy and competency,
- promote positive attitudes in parents about their children,
- help parents understand their children's accomplishments,
- help parents understand the philosophy of the program and the goals of the activities used in each class,
- help parents to appraise health and safety issues and in particular to understand their responsibility for supervising young children when they are near water, and
- promote positive group interactions among the children and their parents.

These dimensions of the teaching task can be more easily appreciated when teachers understand children's behaviour and development and the role that parents and adults normally play in this development. This chapter will focus on the social and emotional development of children and explore how interactions with parents and other significant adults influence this development. The chapter also explores how parents can be encouraged to actively participate in the teaching process and helps teachers to value their contribution.

Understanding Young Children's Thinking

Young children think differently from older children and adults: They are more self-centred and make more direct connections in their reasoning. As was discussed earlier, these modes of thinking are egocentric and concrete. Such modes of thinking limit young children's understandings about events and objects in their environment. Young children often come to conclusions that are untenable from an adult's view. Some of the consequences of these forms of thinking are described here in an attempt to help adults understand some of the differences between their own thinking and that of young children.

Egocentric thinking causes children to have difficulty in appreciating more than one perspective at a time. This will often cause problems with understanding about another's point of view. When participating in group activities children do not readily include others in what they are doing or see that the other members of the group need their consideration. They also tend to believe that their feelings and experiences are felt and experienced by others in the group. There may be difficulties when children need to wait their turn or share equipment. Young children will also experience difficulty when asked to copy the teacher's actions, because to correctly interpret an action that has been demonstrated to them they must first put themselves into the physical position of the teacher. Their inability to take the perspective of the teacher means that they are unable to do this. Young children will demonstrate greater success when asked to mirror actions.

Young children's *concrete thinking* means that they cannot see more than one possible relationship between events. Their thinking tends to be limited by what they see. This causes them to make very limited moral judgements and typically jump to conclusions about who did what, etc. They also subscribe readily to a concept of animism and think that anything that moves is alive and anything that does not move is dead. They will often be scared when they are standing at the edge of the pool: movements of the water may lead them to think that the bottom of the pool is moving.

At some swimming pools pictures of creatures have been painted on the bottom in an attempt to make the environment child-friendly. Children may need to be convinced that the bottom of the pool is stable and that the creatures are not alive before they will enter the pool comfortably.

By 3 to 4 years of age children will have a vocabulary of several thousand words, will be speaking grammatically and will usually begin to ask many questions. However, do not assume that young children understand everything that is said in exactly the way it is intended. Children often need visual clues to help them understand what is implied and expected. Physical supports often help in the teaching situation. Toys, hoops and other markers may help children understand more clearly how far they are allowed to go, how deep the water is, and the solid nature of the pool floor. These supports also help the children understand important concepts such as floating and bobbing under.

Understanding Young Children's Behaviour

Infants and young children have a lot to learn about themselves and about how they should conduct themselves in socially acceptable ways. Infants begin life with a fairly simple repertoire for engaging others through crying, smiling and making eye contact. It is relatively easy for most adults to judge whether an infant is distressed or contented, and the role of the adult is basically defined in terms of attending to the infant's needs.

As children develop they are motivated to explore and learn more about their environment and also to test out a range of social interactions. In response to this the adult's role takes on a wider dimension. Adults begin to set limitations and model to children what is expected of them. Whether we plan it or not, children apprentice themselves to the significant adults in their lives and they begin to learn the rules and customs that govern what they see these people do. The feedback children receive from these significant adults helps them define what is acceptable and what is inappropriate, and this has long-term implications for their development. Positive personal characteristics such as competence and independence and more negative features such as aggressive behaviour and dependency on others have been found to be strongly influenced by parenting style.

However, we must not oversimplify this explanation of development. It is important to consider the influence of the child's characteristics on the relationship between the parent and child. A child's behaviour can have a powerful influence on a parent. Children's age, gender, health and temperament will influence their motivations and responses to situations and people. Temperamentally children can be easy, difficult or slow to warm up, and these characteristics will impact on the interactions between them and their parents. The 'goodness of fit' between infant temperaments and parenting behaviour will determine whether the outcome is healthy or not. For example, a difficult infant may develop well with a parent who is able to cope with the infant's demanding nature. The same type of infant may perform poorly when parents lack confidence or patience. This 'goodness of fit' also explains some of the different responses teachers have to students and is something that teachers need to be sensitive to. Children who are consistently happy and have a good energy level will elicit more positive responses than children who are overactive and non-compliant or who are withdrawn and show little response.

Teachers have a responsibility to be sensitive to and respectful of the needs of infants, children and their parents. Children who present with difficult behaviour need more insightful management. The parents of these children also need support and encouragement. Teachers need to maintain a positive learning environment for all and to make sure their influence on the relationships between parents and their children is positive and supportive.

Children learn important information about themselves through their interactions with adults. These interactions influence their feelings of self-esteem and self-efficacy. Children with good self-esteem have feelings of self-worth and believe in their capacity to contribute to the group. Children with self-efficacy have a sense that 'I can do it' and will try something new that requires them to take some risk.

Influences on Children's Social Development

Young children require time to learn to trust and interact with unfamiliar others. Age also influences how accepting young children are of strange adults and children. During the first few months of life infants will distinguish their mothers from others and will usually be comforted more easily by them. These infants will also display special responses to their own mothers, smiling at them more readily and turning to hear their voices. However, infants are also quite accepting of others and do not usually reject strangers.

A marked change in these behaviours is noted by the age of 6 months, when most infants begin to demonstrate more negative responses to strangers. For instance, they will not smile at strangers and will cry if picked up by unfamiliar adults. In addition infants at this age may strongly protest at being separated from their mothers. These behaviours are, of course, designed to keep the most consistent caregiver close by: They do not, however, mean that infants should be ignored by others. Infants at this stage of development benefit from high-quality and consistent relationships with adults outside the close family circle. These interactions promote a sense of trust in infants. High-quality interactions with infants involve the infant-parent pair and include reference to both the infant and parent during conversations and playful interactions. These interactions help infants to relate to strangers from a secure relationship with their parents.

Infants also take quite some time to learn to interact with their peers. It is quite usual, for example, for toddlers in a group to play near each other without making any reference to each other or sharing in what they are doing. It takes time for infants to be able to understand how to go about participating in shared activities. Infants achieve this best when supported in their games and play by adults who take an active role in helping them to join in. The tasks of sharing and turn-taking and playing out roles can only be mastered when infants are able to understand the perspectives of the other participants. This takes maturity and experience before it can be expected to happen easily.

During the first two to three years of life infants and toddlers are learning how to interact with others. At the earliest stages of social interaction infants start to vocalise tunefully with others. They then try out ways of making physical contact and sharing toys. Infants and toddlers will touch each other and 'trade' toys, but they will also grab at things and push, as they are limited in their social skills and don't have the words to express what they want. Teachers can help structure environments to promote success, particularly by making sure there are enough toys and equipment for each infant and child in the class and by understanding how to help children resolve their problems in constructive ways.

It is important to avoid labelling young children as being naughty. It is equally important to understand that young children are learning how to be social and that they will make mistakes. It is how adults go about helping young children negotiate these situations that matters most. The language used and the messages given to children are the only tools available to them for this learning. As children mature adults can begin to reason with them. However, they will be limited in their ability to think through all aspects of a situation. Typically they will focus on only one aspect of a problem. Children's thinking may seem unreasonable, but if teachers take the time to try to understand how a child is viewing the situation, they can appreciate what is limiting the child's thinking. This does not mean that the teacher can change how the child thinks. It will help the teacher to understand the situation from the child's view and then to use an adult strategy for solving it in a manner that is fair, just and respectful of the child.

Promoting Children's Personal Development

Never underestimate the important role adults have in helping young children develop a sense of self-worth and competency, and a belief that 'I can do it'. Children are born to be social beings but need experiences that help them to understand their role in relation to others in their world. As adults guide children towards an understanding of behaviours, their own actions that they model to the children, and the manner in which they speak to them and treat them, will influence how children value themselves and how they see their abilities.

Children's self-esteem can be supported through establishing a sense of belonging and helping them to form effective personal relationships.

Teachers do this when they do the following:

• Welcome children and parents to the group.

• Show that their participation and contribution is valued and give positive statements to the children such as 'You did that well' and 'I can see how hard you tried'.

• Value their cooperative behaviours and thank them for their effort.

• Give them tasks to contribute, such as collecting things together or arranging things. Comment positively on any help they give.

• Help children form interpersonal relationships and support children in developing effective social interactions. This includes helping the children enter small-group play situations. Show them how to express their needs, communicate effectively and resolve conflicts in a constructive manner.

- Listen to them and let them finish their sentences. Adults who engage children in conversations through using words that show interest and affection, and through speaking in a manner that is consistent with their body language, help children to feel that their thoughts and ideas are of value. It is courteous to children to allow time for the conversation to occur.

- Show genuine affection to the children and humour them. Children will smile and laugh when they feel good about themselves.

Children's self-efficacy can be supported by adults who help them feel they 'can do it'.

Teachers do this when they do the following:

- Help children appreciate their competence.
- Praise their efforts and tell them what worked well.
- Avoid focusing on what is wrong. Children are learning and they need feedback on the desired outcome. Children also need opportunities that encourage them to try and to take a risk. However, these experiences will only be positive in situations in which the child is able to make choices, be independent, use his or her own initiative and have autonomy.

- Respect the children through understanding the limitations in their thinking and through creating a positive and accepting environment.

- Understand children's limitations and do not judge them as naughty. Try to see situations from their point of view. This does not mean teachers should give in to it but rather use children's behaviour management techniques that develop children's self-restraint and understanding of others' points of view. The language and the tone that adults use when managing these situations are equally important.

- Provide children with clear statements about the rules and expectations of the program and remind the children of them when necessary. It is equally important, however, to notice and compliment children when they are behaving appropriately.

Communicating With Young Children and Parents

The family provides the main social context in which the child develops; its role in early development cannot be underestimated.

Interestingly, most of the research in this area has focused on the interactions between children and their mothers, although the influence of fathers and siblings is being increasingly appreciated. Family issues include the effect of a child's temperament on parent-child relationships, parenting beliefs, parenting styles and the influence of social support systems outside the family. An infant aquatic program can influence the family in many ways. The feedback parents get from teachers and other group participants can impact profoundly on how parents view their children and their own competence. The goals for a program should stress the importance of developing a positive climate for parents as well as children.

Infant aquatic programs will often be the first major activity parents engage in with their children outside the home. The program therefore provides an important opportunity for parents to experience a close relationship with a teacher. The teacher is in a position to model appropriate behaviour and to explain aspects of children's development to parents. Many families live with considerable stress in their lives and it is surprisingly easy to provide something positive through a smile, with an appreciative comment or through demonstrating to parents a simple procedure that helps them see their child succeed at something.

Implications for Teaching and Learning

Teachers support positive interactions between parents and their infants and children when they do the following:

• Support children's attachment to their parents. Teachers who work with young children need to respect the special relationship that exists between parents and young children. This bond is actively supported when teachers communicate with parents in a manner that helps them understand the expectations of the program as well as how to appraise children's accomplishments.

• Help parents and children to make constructive separations. It is normal for children to feel afraid and uncertain when they leave their parent, even for very brief periods as in an aquatic program. We need to ensure that separations happen only when infants and children are prepared and that we use verbal supports to cue these separations.

• Support parents in understanding the importance of children's feelings of trust, autonomy and initiative in the development of a healthy personality.

Guiding Parents

Trust

Trust is established when the environment is predictable and when there is an acceptance of the individual. Trust is important for all participants. Infants and children will benefit directly from feelings of predictability and a sense that their needs are responded to in a positive manner. An environment that establishes trust in children will also have an important influence on parents. They will see that their child's needs are respected and that the program will give them an important opportunity to learn more about their infant's or child's behaviour through close experience with someone who is approaching developmental issues in a professional and caring manner.

In the aquatic environment teachers help parents to establish trust in children when they do the following:

A child develops concepts about floating and submersion through play with a doll or animal toy.

• Show consistent responses to all children and avoid showing favouritism to any child or parent.

• Are predictable and establish meaningful routines and create a stable environment.

• Show sensitivity to the needs of infants and children by responding promptly to infants' and children's signals of distress and encourage parents to do the same.

• Show genuine expressions of affection, particularly through smiles, eye contact and voice tone, and address both the parent and infant or child.

• Use teaching techniques that encourage play and exploration and permit opportunities for making choices.

• Avoid making competitive and comparative statements about children and their parents.

• Help parents deal with children's fearful behaviour. Fear is a natural response to a perceived threat or loss of security or safety. Infants and young children are very sensitive to the fears in others around them and may begin to react to fears in their parents. Parents should be encouraged to allow their children to express their fears and then reassure them and help them to think of other ways of coping with the situation. Use play to help children master their feelings. For example, a 3-year-old who has not been to an aquatic program before may show strong resistance to putting the face in the water despite the fact that other, more experienced, 3-year-olds in the group are doing this competently. This is a natural fear and parents should be helped to appreciate the value of approaching this situation tentatively using gradual techniques. A child should never be forced to go under the water. It may be useful to demonstrate this activity using a doll or suitable toy and to allow the child the opportunity to play with the doll and submerge it. The child is then able to develop a better understanding of submersion and to be less fearful about trying it. The teacher should also help the parent understand the importance of not reinforcing the fearful behaviour by reminding the child about it and giving comfort to the child at times when she or he is not afraid.

Autonomy

Autonomy is established in children when they feel they can try something without being judged a failure or being shamed in any way. Children are encouraged to try things within an environment that is both physically and emotionally safe. The setting of limits and the method of discipline and comments given back to the infant or child are the keys to development of autonomy. Limits need to be reasonable, safe and consistently adhered to. The child must feel secure to explore without being shamed or criticised for mistakes made.

Teachers help parents to build a healthy sense of autonomy in their children when they do the following:

- Help parents accept individual differences between children.
- Demonstrate ways of praising children when they try.
- Help parents appraise what their child can do.
- Show parents the importance of giving children opportunities to play and try new things.
- Encourage parents to understand the need to set safe and realistic limits for children and how to reinforce these.
- Allow children to learn in an environment that is free of the fear of being shamed, intimidated or forced.

Initiative

Initiative is the beginning of independence and develops when children have an understanding that they can initiate activities and enjoy their own accomplishments.

Teachers can help parents value their child's independence when they do these things:

- Provide opportunities for children to express themselves and to make suggestions that are respected and listened to.
- Let the children experiment with different ways of doing things.
- Allow children to express their feelings about events.
- Praise children's independent efforts and encourage self-evaluation.
- Help parents cope with their children's egocentric behaviour.
- Help children deal with strong emotions such as frustration and anger. Children also need reminders about socially acceptable ways to negotiate with others and how to solve problems. The manner and language used by teachers in dealing with these situations should act as a model to parents and be free of any judgement. Teachers should encourage parents to understand that this is normal behaviour for young children and should demonstrate positive guidance techniques for managing difficulties with young children.
- Model positive guidance techniques to parents at all times. Positive guidance techniques help children acquire a sense of their own self-discipline and responsibility in social interactions.

Teaching, Parenting and Positive Guidance

Parents and teachers all have their own beliefs about children and their own attitudes towards their upbringing. Differences in styles can be appreciated through three different models of interaction. Adults can be permissive, authoritarian or authoritative towards children.

Permissive or indulgent approaches appear to be caring and nurturant. However, such approaches do not place enough demands on the child to comply. The adults are too tolerant, and children fail to take responsibility for their own actions, lack self-control and are overly dependent on others.

Authoritarian or autocratic approaches rely on the external authority of and obedience to the adult and do not pay enough attention to the needs of the child. Parents expect the child to comply with their wishes at all times. Children feel or are seen as failures, as they are unable to make their own decisions.

Authoritative or democratic approaches involve firm reinforcement of rules and high expectations of achievement. Children tend to become more independent when treated in this manner because their individuality and self-expression are valued. Limits on their behaviour give them a safe boundary within which they have freedom to make decisions for themselves.

Authoritarian or permissive approaches to managing children's behaviour do not help them gain a sense of self-control or responsibility, and children can feel they are failures because they will expect to fail. On the other hand, adults who use an authoritative approach are able to be confident, warm and rational and to reason with the children. They will show a realistic belief in children's abilities and help them to achieve. These qualities offer positive guidance for children, who will display more self-direction and independence in their learning.

Teachers can help parents to understand the value of positive guidance techniques when they model appropriate behaviours to parents, such as the following:

• Maintain the self-esteem of children by using positive language and straightforward statements such as 'Try it this way' and 'You worked on that well' and avoiding statements like 'Don't' or 'That's wrong'.

- Show acceptance of emotions of fear and anger and help children to find acceptable ways of dealing with them.
- Maintain the equal rights of all.
- Catch children doing the right thing and praise them.
- Model conflict resolution and negotiation skills. Children will learn to understand that everyone makes mistakes and that it is how we handle them that matters.
- Show an understanding of the developmental stages children go through and acknowledge the limitations that children have in a confident and rational manner.

The Value of Play

Play is an important process in children's learning. Play provides infants and children with opportunities to try out new experiences in an environment that is free of the risk of failure. Play is the means by which young children explore their world and establish social skills. Playful environments are characterised as being safe and supportive of infants' and children's efforts. Infants and children at play are free to explore and try out new ideas through experimentation and repetition. Play will be most productive when it is supported with toys and equipment that are meaningful to the infants and children and when interested adults engage in playful interactions with them. The most effective adult role in children's play is one that supports these efforts by giving physical assistance when needed, listening to children discuss their ideas and helping them to negotiate difficulties with their peers.

In the infant aquatic program playful experiences help to support the following:

- Bonding between parents and their infant or young child. Through play children learn social interaction and cooperation. These interactions promote language and cognition and allow for the safe expression of emotions. The use of rhymes and songs for parents and infants helps to create warm and friendly interactions.
- Interactions between peers. Young children explore their social worlds through playful exchanges with their peers. Initially this is limited through egocentric thought but becomes more successful as children begin to understand each other's perspective. The playful environment that is guided by insightful adults helps to establish successful interactions and promotes children's ability

to negotiate. The aquatic environment supports peer interactions when it is well equipped with toys and other play equipment. In the early stages it is important to ensure that each infant has his or her own equipment. Shared use and turn-taking occur more successfully in the late toddler and preschool stages.

• A trusting pupil-teacher relationship. Teachers who use songs, games and rhymes in their programs and provide toys and other large equipment to develop a setting in which infants and children can participate in playful interactions will promote an atmosphere in which infants and children will feel free to explore and be safe. In these settings infants and young children are stimulated through their own natural curiosity to try out new experiences. They will be able to develop a trusting relationship with their teacher as they experience freedom to learn.

• Confidence in the water. Play provides opportunities for infants and young children to learn about the nature of the aquatic environment. In the earliest stages of an aquatic program infants will focus on different elements of toys and equipment offered and the properties of water. For example, infants may explore the shape of a toy, then begin to explore the effect of the toy on water. Later on infants may begin to explore the effect they have on the water as they splash and blow it. Gradually infants will begin to explore how they move in the water. Infants need opportunities to support all of these playful experiences until they learn about the objects, the water and their own movement in it.

As adults we often take for granted that infants will know about these things. However, the aquatic environment raises many new possibilities for infant learning. Children will need time to explore this world of water and develop concepts about how it works and what they can do in it before they can begin to master aquatic skills. For these reasons even older preschool children who have had no previous experiences in water may need time and opportunities to play in and around the water before they gain confidence to participate actively.

• Aquatic skill development. A skilled teacher can support children's learning by setting up an environment that encourages children to try things out. Aquatic skills are learnt through children's natural curiosity and drive to explore.

For example, a teacher's goal might be to teach an infant or young child to kick. Playful approaches that will support this development will focus on ways to motivate the child to move through the water. A young infant might be supported in the water by the parent, who throws something interesting a short distance away, in front of the child. The child moves forwards when she or he begins a kicking motion. An older child might use a flotation aid for support as the child propels herself or himself through the water to move from one play station to another or to collect toys and take them to a bucket at the side of the pool. A child who can stand in the water might be encouraged to chase after a colourful ball. It will be no time at all before the water resistance will force the child to use the arms and legs to propel herself or himself along.

In each case the infant or child will begin to kick. These approaches will be more successful than attempts to show the child how to kick or through moving the child's legs and telling the child to 'kick, kick'. The astute teacher will also realise that the method of kicking used by the infant or child will reflect his or her developmental stage and that it is more important to provide the stimulus for this activity through play than it is to try to teach the child how to do it. The flutter kick and other actions, like arm use, will emerge with experience and maturation rather than through formal teaching.

Including Parents in the Program

What do parents need?

Parents will have a greater understanding of the nature and goals of infant aquatic programs when they are informed about these points:

• The philosophy and the teaching practices used in the program. Whether parents are active participants with infants or observers of preschoolers, they will be able to support the program through the expectations and behaviours they adopt for their children outside the program. Parents who understand their responsibility for keeping children safe are more likely to take an active role in promoting safety whenever children are near water.

• Child development. Parents are more likely to show positive behaviours towards their children's learning when they understand the time taken to learn aquatic skills and the stages in the progression of these skills.

• The value of play as a mode of teaching infants and young children. Parents will value the methods adopted in the preschool aquatic program when they understand the significance of play in children's learning. Preschool aquatic teachers should take time to explain the purpose of the activities they plan and implement in their programs.

• The child's placement in a group and the progress the child makes. Information about children can be given in class: Teachers can explain what children have achieved and demonstrate progress. Teachers can also give certificates of achievement or a written report at the end of a series of classes. In addition to providing useful indicators of success and progress, these approaches can help parents to celebrate their child's efforts.

• Practical issues concerning the preparation of children for class, including what to bring; clothing requirements, especially for children who are not toilet-trained; and how to judge which class will suit the infant in terms of his or her normal daily routine.

• Medical issues such as guidelines for exclusion of children who are unwell, how to manage problems related to toileting and hygiene and the importance of explaining any special needs.

• Policies concerning payment for classes and arrangements for substitute classes and other management-related issues.

Parents also need time to ask questions. Classes often run one after the other with little time in between. When this occurs there is little opportunity for parents to raise concerns or to ask questions. Communication with parents can be facilitated through

• regular coffee mornings for parents to meet with the teacher,

• a parent information board or a news-sheet (newsletter) to assist in regular communications and to display relevant information and articles about infant aquatic programs,

• an 'outside working hours' session to help include both parents in their child's activity, or

• individual phone contact with the teacher to discuss issues that the parent has concerns about.

Chapter 5

METHODS OF WATER FAMILIARISATION

Introduction

The way in which infants and young children are introduced to and handled in water will greatly influence their acceptance of the environment and their general attitude to the water. Infants and children will feel secure when they are physically supported in the water in a manner that reassures and comforts but does not restrict their movements. This module explains some principles for handling young infants and children at different stages of development. The amount and type of physical support needed will depend on the infant's ability to maintain an upright posture, patterns of mobility and how independent and self-confident they are in water.

The choice of techniques for teaching entry into the water, breathing control, floating, rolling over and self-produced propulsion will depend on children's development and prior experiences in the water. The key physical characteristics of each stage of development presented earlier in this text provide a useful guide for understanding how infants' and young children's needs for support vary with their development.

For instance, during the Newborn stage the infant is unable to sit, stand or walk. This limited postural control means the infant is dependent on the parent for support of the torso and head.

In contrast, the Baby 1 stage is a period during which postural control becomes established and infants learn to sit, crawl and stand. The support given by the parent may now move down the torso towards the hips and may become more relaxed.

The Baby 2 stage is characterised by the development of walking, and this coincides with infants learning to make short bursts of self-produced locomotion. In the water they will glide from parent to teacher or from supports to the parent and begin to propel themselves with arm and leg movements.

Young toddlers run and jump (Toddler 1 stage) and later hop (Toddler 2 stage). During these stages toddlers begin to coordinate paddling and early swimming-type movements with intermittent breathing and so sustain extended periods of movement through water.

At the Preschool stage children gallop and begin to skip and in water they may begin to organise more mature patterns for swimming. Experienced preschoolers may demonstrate a stroke and side-breathing pattern, although their style may not yet be streamlined.

An understanding of these changes will help teachers to provide appropriate support and encouragement for young infants and children as they begin to explore and master controlled movements of their bodies in the water.

Guidelines for Holding Infants and Young Children

The following list provides some general guidelines to help establish handling techniques that support infants and young children and let them explore the water and develop independent control over their movements.

• Keep hands and arms free of watches, rings and jewellery that scratch and catch on clothing.

• Use an open hand and provide enough pressure for infants and children to feel the touch.

• Provide adequate support for the activity but do not restrict children's movements. The amount of postural support given should ensure infants have sufficient control over movements of the head, help them maintain a balanced position and leave their arms and legs free for movement. Very young infants will need to be cradled or held in a manner that supports the head, while older infants, who have good postural support, need assistance for balance only and can be held much lower down the torso.

• Provide balanced assistance through symmetrical holds. One-handed holds may be used with older children who have mastered breathing and body control in the water.

• The strength of the grip used may need to be adjusted to allow for differences in feeling and temperament. For instance, children who are highly nervous may need a firmer and more calming grip than children who are calm and confident.

• Handling techniques need to be supported with a positive body tone and facial expression from the teacher and parent. Infants and young children are sensitive to physical feelings through body contact. They also use facial gestures to gain a sense of the emotional climate. Children will be reassured through personal warmth shown through smiles and caresses. Negative feelings in others may cause them to reject the experience.

• The position of adults in relation to the position of infants and children in the water is important. Adults should be at the same height in the water as their infant or child and maintain face-to-face contact as much as possible.

- The holding technique should permit infants and young children to feel the buoyancy of the water. This happens when their bodies are immersed and they can sense that they are floating. The holding technique should help them maintain balance and equilibrium rather than support their body weight.

- Movement of infants and children through the water should be planned and made clear to them. Confusing and frightening movements should be avoided and all movements should end with a secure position.

- Keep moving through the water. Movement stimulates interest and helps to focus infants' and young children's attention. Movement also enhances the sense of buoyancy by creating water currents that lift the body.

- Movements should be accompanied by simple verbal messages that alert and prepare infants and young children for what will happen. Praise should be given at the conclusion of the activity.

- Letting go of the hold on infants and children should be planned. Infants should be prepared for the experience through simple cues or through explanations of what is about to happen.

- Immersion and movements that involve infants and young children going under water should only occur after breath control has been fully established and cuing strategies have been learnt.

- Separations from parents should be brief at first and only occur at times when infants and young children are happy and relaxed and ready for this to happen. Exchanges that are forced or poorly timed should be avoided.

- Teachers should keep checking that parents are holding infants and young children correctly and that their attention is focused on their children.

- Teachers and parents may wear T-shirts to provide something for young children to hang onto.

Holding Positions

Different holding positions will influence how infants and young children are able to explore the water and gain independence. This section illustrates how different holds facilitate postural control and ensure that infants and young children are able to sense freedom and buoyancy in the water. For example, infants in the

Newborn stage will need to be cradled in their parents' arms. Slightly older infants, in the latter part of the Newborn stage, will enjoy being carried in a vertical position using the carry hold, in which they are given support to the shoulder and torso. A hip hold, where there is support at the base of the torso, is more suitable for older infants, in the Baby 1 and 2 stages, when infants have good control over their posture. The protective hold is secure and provides a good level of support for infants and older toddlers and is most suitable for a range of exploratory activities and games.

Cradling

Cradling is appropriate for infants in the Newborn stage through to the early stages of Baby 1. The newborn infant has virtually no ability to hold the head up and requires this support. The cradling position keeps the infant in a good position for conversation, provides good eye contact with the parent and helps them to gain an understanding that the situation is a safe and secure one. Alternative cradling positions can be used in the bath and include the infant lying on the parent's extended arms or legs. The cradling position may also be adapted for infants during the Baby 1 stage, who often show a strong resistance to floating on their backs.

Infant in cradle position.

Infant being held in the bath.

The Protective Hold

This is a very secure hold and is suitable for infants in the Newborn stage (two months or more) who have established some head control. The infant is held under the chest with the one hand and the chin is supported by the thumb. The other hand supports the base of the torso at the bottom. This hold can be used to support newborn infants in a prone horizontal position and is also useful for moving them through the water or for passing them from the parent to the teacher.

Infants in the protective hold.

Older infant in vertical position.

The protective hold is also useful for many activities throughout infancy and toddlerhood. The hold can become more relaxed to give infants and toddlers more freedom and encourage them to feel the buoyancy of the water. It is useful for activities in which infants need to be held upright and facing away from their parents. It provides a secure grip and can be used with games and songs that involve swinging infants through the water. It is also useful for holding older infants as they travel and explore around the perimeter of the pool.

To ensure an infant is buoyant in this hold, it is important that the infant's bottom rests on the parent's hand and that the parent does not push upwards. The hand that is placed on the chest is the more active hand in balancing, supporting and guiding movements of the infant.

The Carry Hold

The carry hold is for infants who have developed head control but who are unable to sit. In this hold the infant is seated with the legs apart and the inside arm is up over the parent's shoulder, the head level with the parent's head. The parent uses the right arm to support the infant from underneath and at the lower back. Additional support for the back and shoulder is provided by the left hand at the infant's shoulders. The fingers of the left hand are spread out to support the neck and shoulders. This hold is useful for entry into the water and also permits parents to walk with their infants through the water with the infants safely submerged up to the chin. In this position infants can feel their buoyancy in the water. Parents should be at the same height as their infants as they enter the water. In this position parents can make good eye contact and can engage their infants in the activity by talking, singing and gently blowing bubbles in the water.

The carry hold.

The Hip Hold

The hip hold is an adaptation of the carry hold and is more suited to infants in the latter part of the Baby 1 stage and beyond. It is

used with infants who have good postural control through the torso and are almost able to sit or can sit. This is probably the most common carrying position used by parents. The infant is placed on the parent's hip and is supported underneath with one hand while the other hand comes around the infant's back and holds the infant securely at the waist.

Parents should be shown how to move their infants smoothly from the hip-holding position to the other holds suggested in this section. Encourage parents to talk to their infants as they make these changes in position and to tell them what is happening. This is even important for very young

The hip hold.

infants who do not understand what is being said. Very young infants will pick up on the cues and the reassuring tone of their parent's voice.

Changes in position should also be done with respect to the feelings of infants and young children. When children are relaxed they will enjoy the movements and happily engage in the activity. Infants and children who are apprehensive may resist these movements and become distressed, particularly if the movements are away from their parents' bodies. When infants and young children show this resistance they should be allowed to remain close to their parents. Parents can offer encouragement as they smile, talk, blow bubbles and sing songs to the infants.

The Extended Hold

Extended holds allow infants to be held away from their parents. These holds should only be used when infants are relaxed and can cope with being moved away from their parents. These positions promote greater freedom for infants, allowing them to feel more buoyancy in the water. The face-to-face position encourages good communication with parents and enables infants to gain the reassurance they need in these situations. The extended hold initially places infants in a vertical position, which is good for communication. As older infants become more experienced, they will be able to be moved away from their parents onto their backs before being drawn towards their parents. The extended hold is a natural progression from the carry and hip holds. Infants should be moved gently as their parents maintain eye contact and talk and sing to them.

There is an extended hold for newborns (birth to 6 months). This position allows infants to be face-to-face with their parents and to feel the buoyancy of the water. However, because these very young infants have not yet gained control of the movement of their heads, they will need very secure support. The infant's head should be cradled between the shoulders, and the fingers of the parent's hands should support both the back of the head and the chin. This is an excellent position for communication with the parent (through eye contact, smiles, conversations and blowing soft bubbles etc.) and promotes valuable interactions between infants and their parents.

Older infants can be held under the arms. Thumbs should be at the front and the fingers should be splayed out at the back to steady their position in the upright. The infants should be held so that they can feel their own buoyancy. The closeness and face-to-face position with their parents will promote communication and willingness to move into this position. More experienced infants will enjoy feeling their own movement through the water in this position as they are moved back and forward to their parents.

Extended hold for older infants and children who have good head control.

Face-Forward (Prone) Holding

Prone holding allows infants to experience the water in the swimming position while maintaining eye contact with their parents. The holding technique should vary with the age of the infant and the infant's head and postural control. A very young infant in the Newborn stage will need help to hold the head up and to keep the face clear of the water. This position follows naturally from the extended hold and occurs in response to bringing the infant forward into the prone position. As the infant moves forward the thumb will move up the shoulders and the fingers will spread out across the chest, causing the infant to move into a horizontal prone position. The wrists should come together and form a 'V' under the infant's chin.

Face-forward (prone) holding.

When in this position, the infant's body should be under the water. This enables the infant to feel the buoyancy of the water. With experience the parent's grip can become more relaxed and the infant will float more freely. If infants are held up too high, they will feel uncomfortable and insecure. They will also be out of the water and get cold through exposure.

The face-to-face (prone) position also allows the parent the freedom to move backwards while talking to the infant. The backwards movement creates a slipstream and acts to lift and buoy the infant up.

Older infants who have better postural control of the shoulders and upper torso will need less support and more freedom. Infants in the Baby 1 stage will enjoy a prone holding position that supports them at chest level. The infant should be held with the

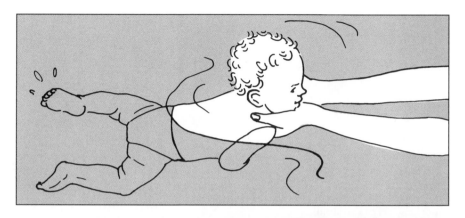

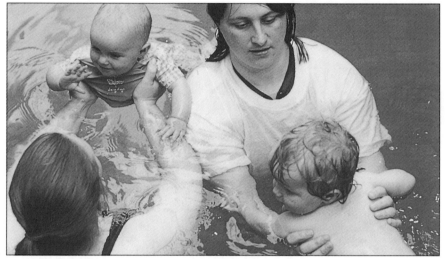

Face-forward (prone) holding, front and back perspectives.

hands to either side of the chest. The fingers should be pointed across the infant's back and the thumbs may be around the shoulders or under the chest. It is important for the parent to keep moving backwards to create a water current that buoys the infant and stimulates the infant's interest in this position. The parent is in an excellent position to provide support through smiles, songs and chatter.

Prone Side Hold

The infant can be turned into the prone side hold from the hip hold, although some practice may be needed to ensure that the changes in the hand positions occur smoothly. The infant is

Prone side hold for young infants, providing maximum support of the shoulders.

Prone side hold for older infants, giving freedom and support.

Splashing and water play encourage arm movements.

brought up against the parent's chest in a front-facing position. The parent then moves the hands to place the left hand under the left arm and the right hand under the right arm of the infant. The hands are placed under each arm with the fingers spread out across the chest and the index finger pointing up to support the chin if needed. Once the grip on the left hand is secure, the right hand can be slipped into place and the infant can be tilted forward.

Infants can travel around the pool with an uninterrupted view and have the freedom to move their arms and legs. It is important, as with other holds, to make sure the infant is held in a position of buoyancy. The infant also needs to feel balanced. The body should be tilted slightly upwards. The parent should be positioned at the same level as the infant and be able to make eye contact. The parent should be encouraged to keep checking the infant's face to avoid accidentally dipping it into the water.

The prone side hold is excellent for infants who are very active. They can be quickly propelled through the water and enjoy some gentle splashing and swishing. Babies can be assisted to track and grasp toys for play and encouraged to kick to get to them. This position can be used with toddlers and preschoolers to encourage reaching out and grasping, to help extend their arm reach and to promote kicking (for example, when they have to make an effort to get to toys placed just beyond their reach).

Sitting Position

The sitting position provides a secure position for the infant to splash the water and to play with toys. The parent should sit waist-deep in water with the child on the lap and encourage the infant to play. With older toddlers this is a useful position for demonstrating arm movements and getting them to 'reach', 'paddle' and 'dig'.

Floating on the Back

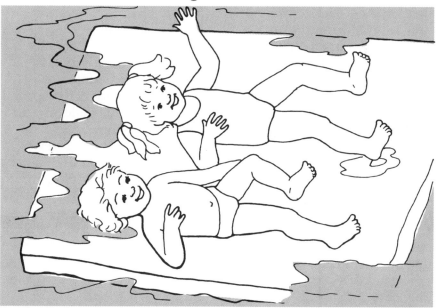

Toddlers and preschool children enjoy a secure introduction to being on their backs in the water.

Pedagogical Issues

The back position has gained a lot of attention in infant aquatic programs. Many references on infant aquatics programs have in the past stressed that this position should be taught as a matter of priority. It has been assumed, for instance, that this position will allow infants some level of safety if they have an accidental fall into water. It is now generally understood that this is not a realistic goal for infants and young children and that they are only safe when responsible adults supervise them at all times in and near water.

However, the issue of the back-float and the methods employed to teach this need to be considered. Questions that need to be raised include: How important is this position for infants and children in aquatics programs? At what age should it be taught? How should our goals for back-floating be adjusted to meet the developmental stages of infants and young children? In particular, how are infants and children encouraged to take up this position voluntarily?

Skill Development

Adults are often surprised to see very young infants successfully float on their backs. Young infants float in a very relaxed and natural way and they do not have to be taught how to do it. This behaviour contrasts strongly with that of slightly older infants of 6 to 8 months of age who are unable to back-float and who generally resist being placed into the back-float position. Infants and toddlers may show a strong resistance to this position for several years. It is not uncommon to see young school-age children show a lot of body tension when they are in this position.

These changes from the very relaxed infant in the newborn period to the resistant older infant and child can be understood in terms of the infant's developmental mastery over upright posture and changes in the infant's buoyancy. Very young infants are able to maintain a back-float position for two reasons. They have above-average buoyancy, due to the relatively high proportion of body fat, and they are unable to roll over or lift their heads when they are placed in the back-float position. To put it simply, when young infants are placed in the water in the back-float position they have no choice but to lie still and to float.

From about 4 months of age infants begin to roll over. They are also beginning to hold the head up and are gaining some postural control over the upper torso in preparation for sitting. As soon as infants begin to gain some control over their posture, they are motivated towards being in the upright position. For instance, when infants at this stage of development are placed on the floor to play, they will typically roll over and push and pull the body into the upright position. When they are able to do this, they will rarely stay on their backs for long. This is particularly evident to parents when their infants show strong resistance to being placed on their backs for changing. They are highly motivated to get to the upright position when these movements are available to them. They do not have to be shown or have these movements explained to them: They are naturally motivated to use the movements as they become available. Thus the newborn floats while the 4- to 6-month-old infant will be motivated to roll and move into a sitting posture. These movements are a natural response. The apparent resistance of infants to being on their backs must not be misinterpreted as stubbornness or loss of an earlier skill.

The early stages of rolling and coming into an upright posture will not be well organised and will result in the infant experiencing considerable difficulty in the water. For this reason infants will need to depend on the adult to assist them with their balance and stability when in the water and will need their support to feel safe and secure.

The methods used to teach the back-float position should consider the child first. Many infants and young children will feel distressed and tense when forced into this position. The back-float position should be introduced with care and concern for the infant's sense of security and well-being. It is recommended that this position should only be introduced for short periods. Parents need to understand the importance of guiding and encouraging their infants into this position using a secure hold and also by giving encouragement through talking, singing and maintaining eye contact. Infants can be distracted by looking at large, interesting mobiles hanging from the ceiling. Flotation mats can be used for a very relaxed introduction to the back position and are especially useful for inexperienced older infants and toddlers.

When back-floating is introduced, it should be within the tolerance of each child and the methods used should provide maximum reassurance and security. The holds should be secure, the activities that are used to introduce this position should be reassuring and the child should have control over what is happening. The child should be praised for any attempts to put her or his head back into the water. A simple counting procedure may help the child begin to gauge when she or he will be returned to an upright position.

The most secure back-float position is for the parent to lay the infant's head on his or her shoulder, with the infant resting against the parent's cheek.

The parent will gradually be able to ease the physical closeness of this hold and let the infant float with her or his head against the parent's chest while supporting the infant's body on one arm and letting the head rest in the other hand.

As the infant becomes more comfortable in this position, the parent can hold the infant by gently placing the hands under the infant's armpits. Infants will be helped to maintain a correct body position in the water if their parents talk to them and encourage them to look straight up into their faces. As the parents walk backwards, the currents will assist the children to float more easily. With repeated experiences parents can gradually ease the fingers away until their infants are floating independently. It is important for parents to remain close by at these times and to be ready to give additional support. It may take some time before an infant is willing to try this without feeling the reassuring touch of the parent's hands.

Back float with baby's head on parent's shoulder.

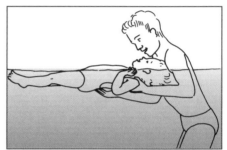

Support along the back can gradually be adjusted to meet the needs of the child.

It is important to appreciate the importance of the infant's own control over the movements of the head when attempting to float. The infant's awareness of the position of the head is crucial for her or his sense of balance and stability. The infant therefore needs to learn to balance her or his own head when floating on the back. Parents should be discouraged from assisting their infants with a head-holding support, as this will promote a false sense of balance and stability.

Emotional security is the key to encouraging infants and young children to take up the back-floating position. Eye contact and a soothing voice will help to make infants more relaxed in this position. Walking backwards will create a current that helps to keep infants afloat.

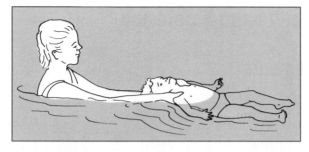

Back-floating with assistance at the shoulders.

Infants and young children need assistance with balancing their bodies while on their backs.

The teacher or parent is ready to offer support as soon as it is needed.

Mobility and Propulsion

Arm and Leg Movements

Early Stroke Patterns

Except for the earliest months when newborns demonstrate the swimming reflex, infants and toddlers rarely use their arms to propel themselves efficiently through the water. Young infants have narrow shoulders and proportionately short arms and typically keep their arms flexed and close to the body. They rely on their kicking to propel themselves along. Effective arm movements would assist them to propel themselves strongly through the water. These movements will develop very slowly and there is no point in attempting to force infants to use large arm movements. Movement should be fostered through early experiences such as splashing and reaching out for toys.

Many infants will swim independently under the water. The stroke pattern involves flexed arm movements.

In the initial stages of self-propulsion infants may use a breaststroke type of pattern and pull with both arms simultaneously. Infants typically use this pattern as they propel themselves under water. As infants progress towards moving on top of the water, they first use short, rapid downwards movements with no back-pulling activity. The body is usually held in the vertical position. The limited arm movements do not propel them along. Toddlers may begin to use greater arm extension and will push downwards and carry this action through to a longer backwards pull. This arm movement is usually accompanied by a more horizontal body position, and the infant is sometimes described as 'dog paddling'.

Preschoolers may move towards using a straighter overarm action and the arms may begin to be raised out of the water. Some very experienced preschoolers may progress to using arms that are mostly extended at the elbow.

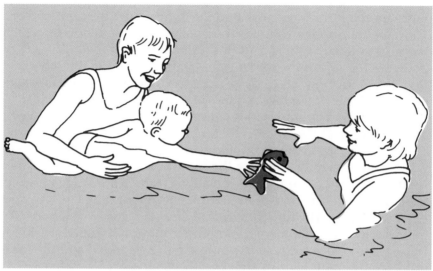

Arm extension can be encouraged through reaching out for toys.

Older toddlers and preschoolers can be shown how to move their arms when sitting securely on their parents' knees. Active cues such as 'reach', 'paddle' and 'dig' can be used with the different movements.

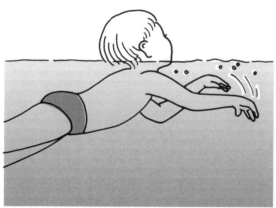

Early arm patterns are characterised by their flexion and short downwards push.

Kicking Patterns

Kicking is present in the reflexive swimming stage of very young infants. Infants do not need to be shown how to kick. They spontaneously kick to propel themselves through the water, although not all infants will demonstrate kicking in their first class.

The kicking movements of the young infant and child, however, are not the classical flutter kick. Kicking movements of infants and toddlers progress through several recognisable stages and start with an action of legs crossing over while they flex and extend. Toddlers then move towards a bicycling type of action in which the hips and legs extend and flex alternately and the body is propelled as the sole of the foot pushes against the water. Preschoolers may begin to show an early flutter-type kick. In the earliest stage of the flutter kick the legs remain bent and the body remains relatively upright. The straight leg flutter only becomes possible when a horizontal body position is assumed.

Changes in leg action cannot be separated from the overall body position and arm action that the infant or young child is using. Infants are in a more upright position in the early stages of self-propulsion, and this position involves a limited range of arm and leg movements. The limbs are flexed and stay close to the body. As toddlers and preschoolers move into a more horizontal position, the arms and legs are able to become more extended and the limb use becomes more mature.

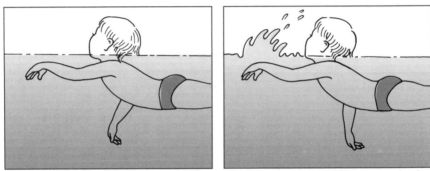

Arm patterns become straighter and move through the water with a greater backwards pull.

It should be remembered that the age at which infants and children are first introduced to aquatic experiences will influence the age at which they will begin to demonstrate these more mature movements. Older children and indeed even adults who have had no prior experiences in the water will demonstrate the more immature and rudimentary arm and leg patterns.

Infants and young children do not need to be taught how to kick; rather, they need to be encouraged to use the kicking pattern that is available to them. It is unnecessary to constantly remind

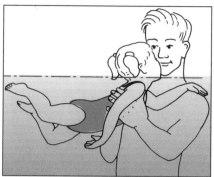

Infants show an upright body position with a crossed-leg kicking action and arms in towards the body.

Older toddlers remain fairly upright and kick with a bicycle or 'pump' action. The arms show a limited range of movement and push downwards.

Toddlers and preschoolers assume a more horizontal body position. The legs may now show a bent-knee flutter (with the toes pointed). The arms are more extended and pull further backwards.

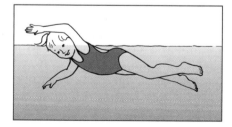

Preschoolers may take up a horizontal body position and swim using a flutter kick in which the legs are extended and the toes are pointed. The arms are extended and used in an early overarm pattern.

them to kick. The best method for getting infants and young children to kick is to motivate them to move through the water. When infants are held in the prone position, for example, parents should be encouraged not to simply propel them along but rather to take them to wherever they try to go when they make an effort. All efforts at moving towards something should be rewarded. Colourful and attractive toys to grasp will motivate these movements. Older toddlers can be encouraged to propel themselves along to collect toys and move around independently or with the assistance of a parent or flotation aid.

Rolling Over and Recovery

The ability to turn and roll in the water in a controlled fashion requires considerable practice before it becomes an independent skill. Infants will initially turn with assistance. Early assisted rolling will help infants to anticipate the feelings of turning and rolling when they are learning to do this for themselves. The type of movement infants use for rolling will vary with their stage of development and their prior experiences in the water. The rolling movement will change as infants move from a vertical body position to a more horizontal one. For instance, in the vertical position infants will need only to flip the head backwards to cause the body to turn upwards so that the feet are raised and they float onto their backs. In the horizontal position infants will need to rotate the head and chest regions in order to get the body to rotate about the horizontal axis.

Teaching rolling movements is often advocated as an important skill in water safety. Turning and rolling in the water are important elements of establishing mobility in the water. They are important as part of a safe entry and exit routine and partial body turning will lead to rotation of the head for coordination of breathing. Developments like these take several years to master. Remember that the goal of infant aquatics is to provide positive experiences for infants and children.

In the preschool years experiences with rolling are important, as they help infants and children adapt their movements to water. Activities like rolling and turning provide opportunities for infants and young children to move through the water using the same movement patterns they have for moving on land. These experiences will also help infants and children to control the balance of their bodies in the water and assist them to gain control of patterns they will need at a later stage for controlled swimming.

Infants' first rolling movement on the floor is from the prone position. Infants initiate rolling by turning their heads. Their bodies then roll over because this movement triggers the action of the righting reflexes that cause the lower body to turn and become realigned with the head. These reflexes are designed to keep the head and body properly aligned and contribute to the development of upright posture. In the water this action can occur with assistance and guidance from the parent. The infant is held in the face-forward (prone) position and is assisted to tip the head back. This will cause the legs to move up and the head to fall back into the water as the body moves like a pendulum through a vertical axis.

Rolling over in the horizontal can only be attempted when infants and young children are happy to be moved onto their backs. As indicated in the photo, this movement can be developed with assistance from the parent. Activities such as rolling off a flotation mat to a parent can also provide a lot of fun and motivation.

Older toddlers enjoy turning on the spot as they move in the water in a vertical or semi-vertical position. This movement can be usefully developed to help infants orient themselves to the side of the pool and to return to it. Older toddlers who are confident in the water will be happy to experiment with a full range of turning and somersaulting movements using large flotation mats.

Rolling over—assisted.

As the older preschooler moves towards a more controlled horizontal position in the water, partial turning of the head can be developed in preparation for controlled breathing.

Submersion and Breath Control

Young infants should never be forced to rely on their airway protective reflex responses when in the water. While it should be acknowledged that these reflexes do prevent water from entering the airways, very young infants are unable to regulate them. In the very young infant the airway protective reflex is so sensitive that it is easily elicited by blowing or splashing water on the infant's face or indeed exposing the face to a cold wind. This is an involuntary response that stops breathing, and it is designed to protect the infant's airways. By about 6 months of age, however, the infant will begin to respond differentially to these stimuli, as the airways protective reflex becomes more integrated with other behaviours involved in feeding and in preparation for speaking. New protective patterns such as coughing give the infant more control over clearing the airways. The emergence of these patterns reduces the urgency to close the airways and the infant gradually tolerates water in and around the mouth, nose and face.

The first six months of life are governed by highly sensitive reflexes that are automatic and cannot be regulated, while the second six-month period is characterised by the beginnings of learned control. Teachers who are trying to encourage learned breath control should remember that breathing is crucial to survival and that any risk of loss of control will raise fears in infants. Fears can be avoided by inviting infants to explore ways of controlling their breathing through modelling and experimentation in structured play situations. In these situations the control should be in the hands of the infants. Their readiness to try out something new should be respected and used as an indicator of progress.

The next section describes the normal progression of breath control shown by infants and young children engaged in aquatic programs. Approximate ages for the mastery of new breath control skills are indicated by the stages of infancy used in this text. It should be noted, however, that the emergence of breath-holding skills will depend very much on the age at which infants and young children are introduced to an aquatic program. In the section that follows it is assumed that infants and toddlers have had continuous experience from an early age.

Infants and toddlers who commence an aquatic program for the first time will need time to develop trust in the new situation as well as an understanding of what normally happens. For these reasons they will need more time to feel comfortable in the water and to find out how to adjust their body reactions in situations that are free of fear. The aquatic teacher needs to understand that beginners at any stage will not be ready to show these behaviours and will need time to master earlier skill levels. Parents should be helped to understand that this is normal. Comparisons between young children should be avoided. Some beginners will move on quickly, while others will need much more time before they feel ready to take on these new challenges. There are no hard-and-fast rules, and the following characteristics are a guide.

Patterns of Breath Control During Early Childhood

Newborn Stage (Birth to 6 Months)

Breath control is reflexive. Typically infants less than 6 months of age will close their airways in response to splashing or blowing on the face. Some infants may be particularly sensitive and may have difficulty regaining their breathing pattern when this reflex is elicited. As indicated previously, this is a protective reflex and serves no purpose in the development of controlled breath-holding. Activities such as blowing on the infant's face and pouring water over the infant as preparation for submersion should not be used with newborn infants. Any preparation such as this should involve the infant as an active participant. This typically occurs at around 7 to 9 months of age when the infant begins to display anticipation and learned responses. Experiences for the newborn should focus on developing an awareness of water around the face and head. Appropriate experiences include

- gently pouring water over the back of the head and towards the side of the face,
- using washcloths and sponges to drip water on the infant,
- encouraging the infant to put the ears under water at bath time, and
- having the infant float gently on the back on a soft mat and letting the water lap around the back of the head and ears.

Young infants can begin to feel the water on their heads and ears as they float on their backs.

Baby 1 and 2 Stages (6-24 Months)

From about 6 months of age infants gain control over the mouth and tongue regions in preparation for eating solids and for articulating speech sounds. At this stage infants may tolerate water in the mouth without reflexively swallowing it. They may actively open their mouths to let the water flow out, or they may take more active steps to spit it from their mouths, or even attempt to blow it out. Anyone who has attempted to feed solids to an infant in this stage will be familiar with the eagerness with which the infant will experiment with these new-found behaviours! Infants in this age group also love to imitate sounds made by their parents. They can be encouraged to blow bubbles in their mouths and on the water.

Blowing bubbles.

Pouring.

Activities to promote breath control at this stage should encourage the infant to play with the feeling of water on the face and mouth through

- pouring water on and around the face;
- playfully blowing and expelling water from the mouth with his or her parent. The parent can foster this through providing visual cuing and support;
- participating in games and activities in which dolls or puppets are used to model submersion; and
- singing songs and chanting rhymes in which infants are cued to prepare to take a breath for a brief or partial submersion (initially for less than one second).

Baby 2 and Toddler 1 Stages (24-36 Months)

The infant or toddler will usually tolerate water on the face for brief periods and begin to learn controlled breath-holding and face submersion. Initial attempts at this may be very tentative, but with encouragement the infant will gradually build up to full submersion for periods of one to four seconds. Teaching methods that promote imitation and modelling with parents continue to be most appropriate in these early stages. As infants become more confident with breath-holding and going under the water, they will be ready to take short assisted glides through the water from teacher to parents and to experiment with brief submersions when they enter the water from a sitting position.

Partial dipping.

Full dipping.

Assisted submerged dipping.

From 24 to 30 months of age infants may be able to integrate breath-holding and paddling movements and move more independently through the water. At this stage infants are stronger and may be able to lift the upper body and clear the face for breathing.

Toddler 2 Stage (36-42 Months)

Experienced older toddlers may take up a more horizontal position in the water and begin to stretch out the limbs to propel themselves in the water. This leads to learning to breathe from the side. Early sideways breathing will not be rhythmical and will not automatically be to one side. Preschoolers learn how to organise these movements as they are challenged to swim for short distances.

Again, it must be stressed that toddlers who have not had regular involvement in an aquatic program cannot be expected to master the skills seen in more experienced children. The first sessions with toddlers who are new to the aquatic program must be enjoyable and designed to give them the opportunity to feel successful at whatever they attempt. Some toddlers will be very fearful of the water and will resist submerging their faces. These differences must always be respected and the toddlers given opportunities to enjoy the program in ways that are meaningful to them and without any pressure to get their faces wet. A carefully designed program will include activities that gradually lead toddlers into these activities in a natural and positive way.

Preschool Stage (42-48 Months)

The experienced preschooler will have progressed from dipping, breath-holding with gliding and torpedoes, and may now be swimming in a horizontal position with extended arm pulling and extended leg kicking, and with breathing towards the side. Suitable activities to assist in breath control with mobility in the water will include activities aimed at achieving more rhythmical control.

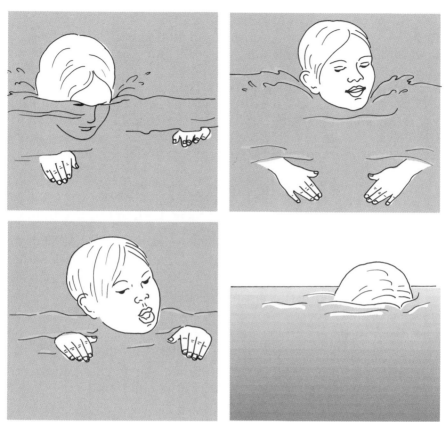

An experienced preschooler may be able to integrate rhythmical breathing into a swimming pattern.

Entries and Exits

An important goal for the aquatic program is to teach infants and young children about how to conduct themselves safely around the pool, including how to enter and leave the water and how to approach the edge of the water. Infants will model safe practices when the desired behaviours are routinely built into the infant aquatic program. Parents can be encouraged to practise these behaviours at home or on other occasions when they take their children near water. It is important to appreciate that water safety is not a single step to be learned. Rather it is an attitude that is built up through repeated experiences in which routines and appropriate behaviours have been established and practised. Over time, the purpose of these practices can be explained in terms that are meaningful to the children.

Safe entry and exit procedures will be mastered gradually. Routines such as entering, turning and getting back to the side and then leaving the water should be built into the lesson plan for entry and exit. Each part of the entry, turning and exit procedure will need to be taught separately and linked into an overall sequence. The method used to teach these sequences will vary with the abilities of the child and the teaching environment. Children who are not able or ready to submerge will need more assistance than children who willingly go under the water.

Guidelines for Teaching Entries and Exits

Teachers can best teach parents and their children to enter and exit the pool safely by doing the following:

- Encourage infants and young children to approach the edge of the pool only when they are with an adult.
- Encourage adults to appreciate the importance of establishing safe routines for entry.
- Ensure the class has a clear beginning and commence the class with the children and parents at the side of the pool.
- The entry procedure should reinforce safe practice and entries should be cued. Parents should invite their children to enter.
- Adjust the method of entry to match the needs of the group and the type and depth of the water. For example, when infants are immobile, they will need to enter the pool in the arms of their parents. The design of some pools will make this difficult, especially for first-time parents. In situations where it is necessary for parents to climb down a ladder, they will need to place their infants safely on a mat near the edge of the pool prior to entry. Alternatively, the infants can be handed to the parents after the parents have entered the water.
- For mobile infants the water entry behaviours should also be taught as part of an entry-exit procedure.
- Infants and toddlers who are mobile in the water should be taught how to get back to the edge and make a safe exit.

Safe Entries for Parents, Infants, Toddlers and Preschoolers

The entry used should reflect the needs of the infant. For example, when a parent with an immobile infant enters a pool with a ladder, he or she should place the infant on a towel or change mat. The parent should then sit down, keeping one arm across the infant to keep the infant safe from rolling, turn and slide into the water, making sure he or she has a safe footing before picking the infant up.

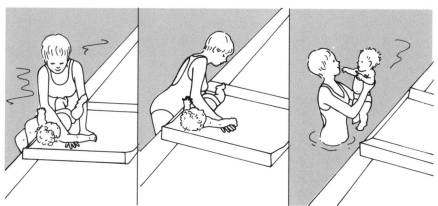

Parents need to learn how to enter the pool safely with their infant.

When an infant can sit well, the parent should begin with the infant sitting next to him or her as he or she keeps one hand across the front of the infant. The parent then turns and slides in, facing the infant. The parent can pick the infant up after the parent has his or her feet firmly on the bottom of the pool. With more experienced infants and toddlers this method can be used to assist them to glide in from a sitting position or to step in.

A safe entry with an infant who can sit.

A parent encouraging a sitting infant to enter the pool.

Toddlers and preschoolers can enter from sitting or standing positions.

Entry From Sitting

As toddlers and preschoolers become more experienced at entering from sitting, they can begin to turn and slide into the pool. Initially they will require assistance from their parents, but they will gradually be able to manage this independently.

Toddlers learning to make a safe entry into the pool.

Entry From Standing

Toddlers and preschoolers can be lifted in or given finger-tip support from their parents.

Assisted standing entry.

The assistance given should meet the needs of the child.

Parent support is ready when needed.

Toddlers and preschoolers can be encouraged to step from the edge of the mat.

Toddlers and preschoolers should be encouraged to move away from the edge of the pool.

Encourage young children to enter the pool safely.

Using the Ladder

The parent should descend first and provide support to the child as she or he descends with her or his back to the parent. Most children will find that they will be able to exit using the ladder before they can enter.

Alternative Methods of Entry

Shallow pools or a beach-style entry provides opportunities for mobile infants to crawl in or walk in with their hands held by adults. When parents are walking in with an infant in their arms, they will need to be advised to slide their feet along to avoid slipping. The additional weight of the infant makes them top-heavy and could cause a heavy fall.

Pools with steps provide opportunities for mobile infants to crawl in backwards.

Deep pools that have a deck at the edge allow infants to sit and jump forward or to crawl in backwards into their parents' arms. Alternatively, a large immersed platform may be placed near the edge of the pool to provide a safe ledge.

Head-First Entries

Head-first entries should be adjusted to the skill of the infant or toddler and can begin with entry from a sitting position. Infants and young children who are not ready for submersion and who are dependent on their parents should make entries directly into their parents' arms. They should not be forced or tricked into going under water.

Assisted head-first entry.

Independent head-first entry from sitting.

Finger-tip assistance for a head-first entry.

Jumping Entries

Young children may be able to jump in safely from the large equipment and then from the sides. Jumping in must be introduced carefully and teachers should make sure that children do not hurt themselves by hitting their backs against the side of the pool or jumping too forcefully and pushing water up their noses. Children should be taught to look before they jump and only to jump on cue. Care should be taken to choose a safe area for jumping and to avoid the corners of the pool.

Infants who are able to cope with submersion but have limited self-propulsion should be given assistance to turn and lift themselves up from the water once they have entered and submerged, and then to glide back to the edge of the pool. The amount of assistance given should be adjusted to meet their needs. Parents who bring their children up face-to-face to make immediate eye contact and give smiles and praise will positively reinforce these behaviours and build their children's sense of success.

Immature head-first unassisted entry.

Standing infant—unassisted jumping.

The child should be encouraged to jump forward.

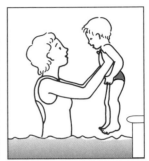

Infants should be guided through safe entry, turning and exiting procedures.

Independent entries such as jumping and diving in should only be attempted when children can confidently submerge and are able to bring themselves up, turn around and propel themselves to a parent or back to the side of the pool. Safety rules must be taught and enforced at all times. Children must be taught to wait for a cue before jumping or diving into the water.

Exits

Exploration of the sides of the pool should be systematically introduced into the program from an early age. This can be encouraged by having young infants collect and bring toys to the edge of the pool. Parents can then assist them to hand-walk along the edge of the pool. Toddlers and preschoolers can be encouraged to bounce up and lever their bodies out of the water at the edge of the pool. As the children become stronger they will take their own body weight through their arms and lever their bodies up out of the pool into a crawling position.

Infant being assisted to explore the edge of the pool.

Infant at the edge of the pool making an independent hand-walk.

Child learning to lever her weight up and climb out.

Flotation Aids

A large variety of flotation aids is available. The goal of the program should, however, be clearly defined in terms of children being able to master the water environment on their own. The use of flotation aids should not create any dependency. Infants and children should be able to enjoy the aquatic environment with and without flotation aids.

Parents should be reminded that flotation aids are no substitute for *constant supervision* when infants and young children are in the water.

Flotation aids are sometimes used as they may

- provide variety,
- promote relaxation,
- assist in developing self-propulsion and coordination of the arms and legs,
- encourage exploration and experimentation, and
- add colour and interest.

Flotation aids need to be selected carefully to provide support without unnecessary restriction. Some aids may make it more difficult for infants and toddlers to use their arms or experience their own sense of balance and manoeuvrability in the pool.

Points to consider when choosing flotation aids:

• Some aids provide too much buoyancy and cause infants to tip head-first into the water.

• Some aids are too restrictive. For example, arm attachments can make it difficult for infants to use their arms and may leave them floating without any appreciable control.

Teachers need to make sure that parents and children do not become too reliant on flotation aids.

Flotation Mats

These are an excellent aid for all ages and can be used in many ways to vary the program. Soft flexible mats are useful for infants and preschoolers and can be used to introduce them to water gradually. Water will lap gently around them as they lie on the mats, sit on the mats, or even attempt to crawl or stand and walk on the mats. Rigid mats provide a more secure base and are excellent for activities associated with seated entries, stepping into the pool and rolling in. Combinations of rigid and flexible mats can provide a challenge for infants and toddlers who need to feel more support before they will play on the less secure surface and then enter the water. Mats also provide an excellent focus for group activities.

Mats are also great motivators for young children who are learning to glide, paddle and swim short distances. The mats can be stationed around the pool to provide stations for them to get to. Platforms and other large equipment also provide excellent alternatives, particularly when the water area does not have sufficient shallow space for class activities.

Care must be taken to ensure infants do not slip off the mats, especially when near fixed obstacles or pool edges.

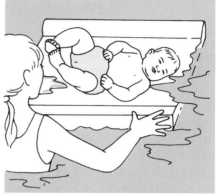

Flotation mats encourage independent exploration and play in the water.

Mats provide an opportunity to float independently on the back and gradually feel the water on the body.

Group play on a flotation mat.

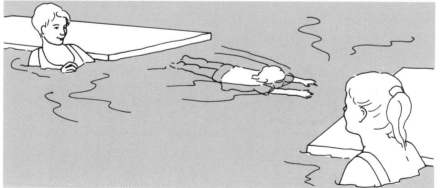

Flotation mats provide additional support for activities such as gliding and torpedoing through the water for short distances.

Toys and Other Equipment

The choice of toys that can be brought into the pool environment is limited only by the teacher's imagination. Children will naturally be drawn to explore the aquatic environment through play with toys and other colourful equipment. Toys are useful for younger infants to explore the properties of water through pouring, splashing and watching toys float or sink. They are very useful in getting infants and children to reach out and extend their arms, or to kick to get to where the toys are, or to climb up at the edge of the pool for toys that are just out of reach. Toys are good distracters for children who are unsure and need more time to play in the water before they are prepared to learn to master their own body movements in it. They are helpful in developing themes and making the program more interesting and appealing to children.

Toys must be carefully selected to ensure that they are safe and appropriate for the age group. Toys must be free of sharp edges or small pieces that can come off and be put in the mouth or breathed in. They should be made of solid materials that will not break or shatter. Toys must be emptied of all water, rinsed and stored in open containers in a dry spot. Always check each toy for safety before using it again.

Children need opportunities to explore the properties of water.

Finding out about water.

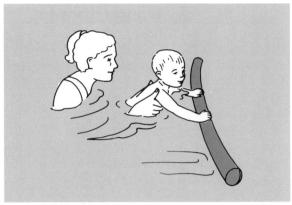

Learning to balance in the water.

Some children need extra support to encourage them to move in the water.

Children enjoy playing in the water.

Chapter 6

PROGRAMMING

Introduction

Successful programming for infant and preschool aquatics is dependent on the insight and skill of the teacher. Teachers who understand that young children's aquatic skills emerge through interactions with their parents and each other will provide opportunities for skill development through play and exploration. These teachers will also be realistic about the time period over which skills emerge and appreciate differences in the aquatic readiness of each infant and child. Most importantly, these teachers will be flexible and ready at any time to adapt the program to meet the needs of individuals.

The issues raised in each of the chapters presented are intended to help teachers appreciate the developmental principles that should be used for planning. There is no prescriptive course for infants in aquatic programs. Infants at any particular age will vary enormously in aquatic abilities. A skilled teacher will assess each infant's and child's developmental readiness for aquatic skills and will be able to adapt the program to meet their needs. Quality infant aquatic programs will also ensure that the experiences planned for infants and their parents are enjoyable and conducive to learning.

The effectiveness of infant and preschool aquatic programs will be indicated by children's willingness to continue with aquatic activities beyond the preschool years and through an improved sense of water enjoyment and safety. This is likely to happen when the infant and preschool aquatic program is based on a developmental perspective that recognises individual differences among infants and appreciates their need to learn through playful interactions with adults who are caring and responsive to their needs. Parents who engage in these activities are more likely to be aware of the characteristics of young children and in consequence have a greater awareness of their own responsibility for their child's safety in and around water.

Lesson Plans

A lesson plan will help to ensure that each session has a predictable format and that activities are selected from each of the major skill areas. A lesson plan will also help to ensure that routines and activities that support water safety and parent education are planned for.

Examples of lesson plans are included at the end of this chapter for each of the main stages of infancy and early childhood. The plans have been adapted to reflect the general levels of skill that can be expected to be mastered by each age group (Baby 1, 6-12 months; Baby 2, 12-24 months; Toddler 1 and 2, 24-42 months; and Preschooler, 42-48 months).

This checklist helps identify the types of skills infants and young children are ready for. These activities will provide beginner teachers with a starting point for planning.

Checklist for Lesson Plans

Skills	Parent skills	Activity	Equipment
Entries			
Beach	Carry hold, careful stepping		
Slide in	Positioning and guarding infant	From side of pool	Thick towel or mat for infant
Sitting	Varying assistance from holding torso to finger-tip	From side of pool or from large mat	Large mats
Standing	Varying assistance through to finger-tip	From side of pool or from large mat	Hoops
Jumping	Varying assistance	From side of pool or from large mat	Large mats
Diving	Varying assistance	From side of pool	
Breath control			
Surface	Modelling	Blowing	Ping pong balls
Submersion			
Chin	Modelling and demonstrating prone hold	Moving on stomach	Small toys that float
Ears	Eye contact with infant as infant floats on back Vertical hold	Lying on back	Suspended toys to see
Mouth	Modelling prone and vertical holds	Blowing and submerging	Mirror
Face and eyes	Modelling prone and vertical holds	Submerging with parent	

(continued)

(continued)

Skills	Parent skills	Activity	Equipment
Whole head	Modelling carry hold	Play with parent	Submerged toys to fetch (from bottom of pool)
Floating and balance			
On back	Support of whole body and head gradually being reduced to support of the shoulders	'Twinkle, Twinkle, Little Star'	Large toys suspended from ceiling
On stomach	Prone holding		Toys to fetch
Turning and rotating	Assisted rolling from back to front	'I'm a Little Pancake'	
Self-propulsion in shallow water			
Walking	Hold hand as needed	Forwards and backwards	Toys to fetch/races
Running	Hold hand as needed	Forwards and backwards	Toys to fetch
Jumping	Hold hand as needed		
Hopping	Hold hand as needed		
Self-propulsion in deeper water			
Torpedoes	Provide a point of recovery	Moving from base to new station	Large mats to provide stations, personal flotation aids as necessary
Sculling	Be near and help if needed	Moving along on the back	Under an arch Toys on ceiling
Swimming movements	Provide a point of recovery	Moving across pool or from base to new station	Large mats to provide stations, personal flotation aids as necessary
Exit			
Explore edge of the pool	Protective hold	Toys to look at or to place or grasp	Wide selection of toys

Skills	Parent skills	Activity	Equipment
Hand walk along the edge of the pool	Protective hold as needed	Toys to look at and grasp from edge	Toys
Lever body up at edge of pool	Protective hold as needed	Toys to look at and reach	Toys
Climb out at edge of the pool	Support as needed	Include in entry, turn and return to edge routine	
Using steps	Be near to give help if needed		
Using ladder	Stand behind infant to give help if needed		
Water safety			
Use routines	Understanding of importance of routines	Encourage children to watch and wait for cues	
Parent education			
Vigilance	Always monitor child	Teacher models	
Encouragement and praise	Maintain eye contact and provide positives whenever possible	Teacher models	
Role as teacher	Engage their child through play	Teacher reinforces	

It is assumed that these age groups have had regular involvement with infant and preschool aquatics programs. In cases where infants and young children have not had prior experience, the program should be adapted to meet their needs.

Teachers should ensure beginners at any age level have an opportunity to become familiar with the routines and expectations of the program and comfortable in the aquatic environment. Some children will feel more comfortable taking time to observe before they join in the activities.

Lesson plans are essential. They help teachers to

- set goals that are appropriate for the aquatic readiness of the group,
- plan to meet the needs of each infant or child in the class,
- prepare any newcomers to the group,
- select learning experiences that provide for a balance between activities that encourage consolidation of previous skills and extend skill development,
- identify the skills that parents need to know in order to support the activities,
- select an appropriate range of toys, games and songs to support the learning activities, and
- determine the lesson format and the order in which the activities are introduced.

A teacher who has a clear plan for each lesson will also be in a better position to adapt activities to meet individual requirements of infants and children.

Teachers will need to give consideration to practical issues such as the following:

- Class size and the number of participants.
- How much equipment is required and where it needs to be placed for the smooth running of the class.
- Routines for the beginning and conclusion of each session. These help young children understand the order of the class and help teachers build water-safe practices with parents. For instance, when parents and children meet at a point that is away from the water, good routines are established for entry procedure and children's regard for the edge of the water is supported. Routine activities for introducing new members to the group and for a regular farewell activity promote a sense of belonging to the group.
- Goals for the lesson. The goals for a particular class should be considered within broad goals. For example, when a teacher is working with a group of parents and infants for the first time, the most important part of the class will be the entry procedure. This might be followed with some activities to promote awareness of movement in the water and conclude with play. As the confidence of the parents and infants in the class increases and they become more relaxed, the focus of subsequent sessions shifts towards greater exploration of movement through the water and experimentation with breathing.

- The lesson format and the allocation of time for each activity. The short attention span of infants and toddlers means that most activities should be planned for no more than a few minutes. The order of activities will also need to be planned to ensure that there is a good transition to each new activity and that any toys and equipment that are needed are in the right place at the right time.

Programming for Each Key Age Group

Newborn Stage (Birth to 6 Months)

In the bath at home, no formal program is recommended.

Goals

For newborns to

- experience the sensation of their bodies in the water,
- tolerate water being poured over the back of the head,
- enjoy playful experiences with parents in the bath at home,
- feel relaxed in the aquatic environment,
- experience prone and supine positions in the water, and
- begin to play with and explore the water.

For parents to

- enjoy playful times with the infant in a warm bath at home,
- observe the infant's responses to the water,
- introduce the infant to the aquatic environment in a manner that is respectful of the infant's immaturity,
- gain confidence in handling the infant in water, and
- understand that an infant in a bath must be supervised by a responsible adult at all times.

Bathtime can provide many opportunities for infants to play with and explore the water, as well as gain a sense of their own body movements.

The daily bath routine can be easily adapted and time for water play and familiarisation can be planned prior to introducing shampoo or soap in the water. Some extra preparation may be necessary, particularly in ensuring that the room is adequately warmed for an extended session of water play and that there are plenty of towels available for both the parent and the infant.

Newborn infants will find the baby bath tub most satisfactory for an aquatic experience. A small back support can be used to help support the infant in a reclining position. A back support will ensure that the infant is stable and won't roll. The parent is free to play and offer toys for the infant to grasp. Young infants will usually tolerate lying in the water with the back of their head and ears under the water.

The large bath will provide opportunities for parents and infants to bathe together. In a deep bath infants can gain a sense of buoyancy as the parent cradles them and lowers them into the water until their bodies are fully immersed. Parents can place their infants in various positions, such as on their backs resting on their parents' legs. At around 3 months infants will begin to enjoy being placed on their stomachs in shallow water in the family bath. They will be able to grasp at toys floating in the water. A foam wedge or thick towel can be placed in the bath for texture and support.

Parents should never force their infants to put their faces in the water or to submerge their heads. It is sufficient for infants to experience water being poured on the back of their heads and over their ears. Parents can be encouraged to pour water gently over the back of infants' heads and to position them in the water so that their ears are submerged. The goals of these early experiences should be to help foster an awareness of the sensation of water. The tolerance of infants to these activities should be a guide to parents. The infant's sense of comfort and security should be considered above any other goal. Parents also need to be aware that they must *never* leave an infant in a bath unattended or in the care of a sibling. Parents must always wrap the infant in a towel and take the infant with them if they need to leave the room for any reason.

Baby 1 Stage (6-12 Months)

Goals

For infants to

- become familiar with activities in an aquatic environment,
- feel secure and content in the water,
- gain a sense of buoyancy and to sense the movement of their bodies in the water,
- tolerate water around the chin and mouth area,
- gain experiences in water in different body positions including prone, supine and vertical,
- explore the water environment through play and exploration with a range of toys,
- experience independent movement in the water environment through the use of flotation aids and large equipment with parental assistance,
- become familiar with routines that promote an awareness of the edge of the pool, and
- participate in small group activities with the assistance of their parents.

For parents to

- learn how to enter and hold their infant in the aquatic environment, using techniques that are safe and promote a sense of security in their infant,
- understand basic requirements for the health and safety of young infants in the water,
- engage with their infants in playful interactions that promote their infant's confident exploration of the water, and
- appreciate their role in providing a safe, secure and enjoyable aquatic experience with their infant.

Infants in this age group will develop rapidly, and many may progress quickly from being fully supported in their parents' arms to happily exploring the pool environment independently when supported by parents in a flotation aid (such as a swim ring, backpack or singlet (sleeveless) top with flotation blocks). Flotation in the supine and prone positions will require parent support or the use of a flotation mat. Entry skills will probably commence with the infant lying down at the side of the pool as the parent enters first, before picking the infant up.

Towards the end of this period many infants will be happy to sit at the edge of the pool and fall in to the tune of 'Humpty Dumpty Sat on the Wall'. Some infants may step on cue from the side of the pool with assistance from their parents. With increasing mobility infants may begin to crawl or walk to their parents along a flotation mat. Balance in the water can be explored with flotation aids such as arm wings and backpacks.

As infants move from 7 to 9 months they will begin to anticipate events and remember simple routines. Some infants may begin to consciously prepare themselves for submersion and show greater tolerance for putting their faces in the water or dipping their mouths and chins in. They quickly learn to follow cues such as 'one, two, three' or 'we all fall down' (as in 'Ring a Ring o' Roses'). Some infants may be happy to submerge themselves completely in playful exchanges in which they imitate their parents.

Exploration of movement in the water can be encouraged in prone, supine and vertical positions as parents hold their infants and move through the water. Toys will provide useful motivators for infants to grasp and may prompt infants to kick to move closer to them. As parents move their infants around the pool and explore the sides, they can encourage the infants to climb up at the edge in preparation for learning a safe exit procedure. Infants who are mobile can be encouraged to climb out (to get a favourite toy, for instance). Towards the end of this period many experienced infants may begin to exit the pool and climb up the ladder with assistance.

Infants at these stages imitate their parents in songs and games. Parents and teachers can demonstrate desired behaviours using dolls, puppets and toys for infants to observe.

Baby 2 Stage (12-24 Months)

Goals

(to build on the goals of previous stages as appropriate)
For infants to

- explore the water more independently, returning to their parents as a source of secure and reliable support as needed,
- make a variety of assisted entries into the water,
- explore methods of propulsion through the water with and without assistance,
- move towards independent submersion of the face,
- use flotation aids to assist with independent movement in the water,
- be introduced to routines that promote awareness of safe practices when in and around the water environment, and
- socialise with their peers in small group situations with assistance from their parents.

For parents to

- understand their role in maintaining vigilance at all times when young children are in or near the water,
- provide assistance that is appropriate for the needs of their child for entry, support and movement through the water and for exiting the pool, and
- praise and encourage the child's efforts towards independence.

Infants in this age group are becoming mobile and are ready to begin to explore their own movement through the water. Independent movement will tend to be upright at first, although more horizontal movements with paddling movements of the arms and legs with breath control in the mid-line are usually evident at the end of this stage. Entry skills may include assisted standing and independent standing entries. These can be safely explored in the pool with the aid of flotation mats. Parents can assist their children to begin gliding through the water from mats and the edge of the pool. Routines such as entry, turning and exit procedures will be established.

Greater independence and mobility may mean that many infants are ready to engage in circuit-type activities. Circuits provide motivation as children are encouraged to move from point to point and participate in a new and interesting activity.

This age group will be motivated by a wide range of toys and themes and will enjoy opportunities to play in the water and to observe its properties, for example, when pouring and tipping from container to container. Most infants find water play to be a soothing experience. This age group also enjoy nursery rhymes and songs and will begin to join in and follow simple action songs, particularly when assisted to do so by their parents.

Toddler 1 and 2 Stages (24-42 Months)

Goals

For toddlers to

- gain greater independence in aquatic skills,
- learn safe entry and exit procedures,
- further integrate breath-holding skills,
- move towards self-propulsion,
- explore a wide range of manoeuvres in the water, including turning and rolling,
- move towards development of arm and leg actions,
- interact with the teacher and peers in group activities and to depend less on their parents,
- become more aware of the depth of the water and confidently move in deeper water, and
- learn routines and skills that encourage safe practices in the water environment.

For parents to

- learn to adjust the amount of support given to their child so that the child can explore the water more independently,
- provide appropriate guidance and praise to support their child's competence and confidence in the water, and
- appreciate their responsibility for the safety of their child.

Entries may now include jumping independently and assisted head-first entry. Playful activities such as walking, running and jumping through the water will help them gain greater control over their movements in the water and refine their sense of balance.

Rotation and turning skills can be extended. Breath control may be integrated rhythmically with self-propulsion, and children may be able to move independently over greater distances. Self-propulsion may also include activities in deeper water.

Children will enjoy circuit activities that encourage them to move around the pool from station point to station point. At the conclusion of this stage many toddlers may refer only briefly to their parents for assistance and they may be able to engage in group activities with their peers and teacher for extended periods.

Preschool Stage (42-48 Months)

Goals

For preschoolers to

- be independent and confident in the water,
- further integrate their breath control and propulsive action,
- take responsibility for participating in the class routines,
- continue to develop concepts about personal water safety, and
- experience simple safety procedures such as getting to the side or being pulled to the side.

For parents to

- provide effective support for their child's independent efforts and
- appreciate their responsibility for the supervision of young children at all times they are near the water.

Preschool children can be expected to show wide variation in their aquatic readiness levels, and this will depend very much on their previous water experiences. Preschoolers who have no prior experiences in the aquatic environment will not be ready to begin at the same level as more experienced preschoolers. Program development will need to reflect the goals set for the toddler groups. It will be necessary to plan to introduce newcomers in a manner that respects their level of aquatic readiness. Personality factors and other child-rearing factors will also influence children's willingness to get into the water and try out new experiences. A child who is very shy and timid may need to begin with a simple entry and be given time to play in the water.

Experienced preschoolers may be ready to explore all methods of entry. It is important to ensure that all entries are attempted in safe situations and in a calm and responsible manner. Movements through the water may be explored through walking, jumping and hopping, and self-propulsion may now be developed through to a horizontal body position. Skill development may be focused on more directly by encouraging torpedoes, sculling and back-floating. Breath control may be voluntary and can be developed into a rhythmical pattern that is integrated with the movements of the arms.

Circuit activities are a useful means of providing interest and can be used to challenge preschoolers to test themselves and extend their levels of competence. Preschoolers are also becoming more self-aware and may be able to handle concepts of water safety. However, they will continue to require supervision when they are in or near water at all times. Parents must understand that these activities are introductory and must not relinquish the parental role and the responsibility to ensure their children's safety.

Songs and Games

Songs and games help establish routines for infants. Songs provide useful cues for skills and also help promote a social atmosphere for infants and their parents. For instance, with a young group of inexperienced parents and infants, a song such as 'Look at My Baby Sleeping' will help parents to gain confidence in holding their infants in a cradle hold and moving through the water. The infants gain a sense of being moved through the water in an activity that promotes a close relationship with their parents. Songs also encourage parents to engage with their infants in a playful manner and promote parent confidence and acceptance in the group.

When working with toddlers and preschoolers, teachers will find that songs and games can prompt their imagination and provide a source of motivation for exploring movement in the water as children 'move like a whale' or 'jump like a frog'. Children will join in and carry out the actions of their favourite songs, and they may be happy to participate in a small-group setting. The songs chosen should prompt actions and movement. The examples provided are a guide for songs, rhymes and group activities in the infant and preschool aquatics class. Beginner teachers may find them a useful start. Parents and infants may have their own that they would like to share.

Examples

'What Do You Think My Name Is?' for getting to know each other

'Look at My Baby Sleeping' for cradling and moving baby in the water

'It's Raining, It's Pouring' for activities with water over the back of the head

'Teddy Bear, Teddy Bear, Turn Around' for rotating and group games

'Here We Go Round the Mulberry Bush' for group activities moving through the water

'I'm a Little Pancake' for turning over

'Ring a Ring o' Roses' for steps to submersion in group activity

'Ring a Ring o' Roses (We All Wave 'Bye)' for group farewell

'Humpty Dumpty' for entry from side of pool or from large mat

'Little Green Frog' for jumping and moving through the water

'If You're Happy and You Know It' for a group game and farewell

'Down by the Station' for moving through the water

'I'm a Dingle Dangle Scarecrow' for fun get-together and body awareness

'The Motors on the Boat' (to the tune of 'The Wheels on the Bus') for movement through the water

'Five Little Sausages' for group games such as rolling off a mat into the water

'I'm a Little Teapot' for group fun and movement

'Twinkle, Twinkle Little Star' for floating on the back

Lesson plan: Baby 1
Age group: 6-12 months
Ability: Beginners
Class day/time: Tuesday, 10 AM
Number of participants: 5

Skills	Focus	Parent skills	Activity	Supporting equipment & songs	Time
Entry	Ladder entry	Place and guard infant	Place infant safely and climb ladder	Towels/mats	1–2 mins
Social greeting	Group	Help infants to greet each other by name	'Hello' song	'What Do You Think My Name Is?'	3–4 mins
Floating and balance	On back	Cradle hold	Parent cradles infant in water until body is bouyed	'Look at My Baby Sleeping'	3–4 mins
Self-propulsion	On stomach	Parent using prone forward hold faces infant and talks to encourage him or her	Walking around, creating a current to buoy the infant	Floating toys for interest	2–3 mins
Breath control	Surface	Hip hold, keeping infant's head level with parent's	Parent blows on infant's hand and on the water		2–3 mins
Steps to submersion	Back of head and sides of face	Hip hold	Parent dribbles water from sponge	'It's Raining It's Pouring'	2–3 mins
Free play	Toys to fetch	Prone hold and care to monitor infant's mouth	Collect toys and put on flotation mat	Floating animal toys	3–4 mins

Skills	Focus	Parent skills	Activity	Supporting equipment & songs	Time
Goodbye routine	Group	Parents to join in actions	Vertical hold and parent moves infant into centre of group	'Teddy Bear, Teddy Bear, Turn Around'	2–3 mins
Exit	Ladder	Manage infant and ladder safely	Parent places infant on towel	Towels	

Times are suggested only. Teachers should be ready to adapt a lesson plan and extend or shorten segments according to levels of interest and enjoyment.

Lesson plan: Baby 2
Age group: 12-24 months
Ability: Moderately experienced
Class day/time: Thursday, 2 PM
Number of participants: 4

Skills	Focus	Parent skills	Activity	Supporting equipment & songs	Time
Entry	Climb in	To assist as needed			1–2 mins
Social greeting	Group	Parents to help infants to greet each other by name	'Hello' song	'Here We Go Round the Mulberry Bush'	3–4 mins
Floating and balance	On back and rotation to stomach	Parents assist as needed	Looking up to ceiling, rotating when ready	'I'm a Little Pancake'	3–4 mins
Self-propulsion	In shallow end of pool	Parents assist as needed	Walking, running across the pool	Rings to hold	2–3 mins
Breath control	Under water	Blowing out on submersion	Parent blows with infant	Encourage noisy blowing	2–3 mins
Submersion	Steps to full submersion	Parents model for infant	Picking up toys from shallow water	Rings to grasp	2–3 mins
Free play	With peers	In shallow water flotation mat provides work bench at appropriate height	Free play with toys on flotation mat	Selection of toys for pouring, fitting and stacking	3–4 mins
Goodbye routine	Groups	Parents to join in actions	Actions and song	'Ring a Ring o' Roses...We All Wave 'Bye'	2–3 mins
Exit	Steps	Parents assist if needed			

Lesson plan: Toddler 1
Age group: 24-36 months
Ability: Moderately experienced
Class day/time: Wednesday, 11 AM
Number of participants: 8

Skills	Focus	Parent skills	Activity	Supporting equipment & songs	Time
Entry	Standing	Assist as needed	Stepping in at edge of the pool	'Humpty Dumpty'	1–2 mins
Social greeting	Group	Parents help toddlers to greet each other by name	'Hello' song	'Little Green Frog'	3–4 mins
Floating and balance	On back	Parents assist as needed	Looking up to mirror held by parent	Mirrors	3–4 mins
Self-propulsion	Kicking	Parents assist as needed	Using kickboards to go across the shallow end of the pool	Kickboards	2–3 mins
Breath control	Under water	Blowing out on submersion	Parent blows with toddler	Looking in the mirror with parent	3–4 mins
Steps to submersion	Entry and steps to full submersion	Parents assist for recovery	Entry from the mat and swimming through the hoop to parent	Hoop	2–3 mins
Free play	With peers	Taking toys for mat across to the side	Toys on flotation mat	Selection of toys for floating and pushing across the water	3–4 mins
Goodbye routine	Group	Parents to join in actions	Actions and song	'If You're Happy and You Know It'	2–3 mins
Exit	Ladder	Parents assist if needed	Climbing out independently		

Lesson plan: Toddler 2
Age group: 36-42 months
Ability: Experienced
Class day/time: Monday, 11 AM
Number of participants: 4
(parents as observers)

Skills	Focus	Activity	Supporting equipment & songs	Time
Entry	Entries	Wade-in entry	With and without partner	1–2 mins
Social greeting	Group	'Hello' song Children to greet each other by name	'Down by the Station'	3–4 mins
Floating and balance	On back	Formation with feet to centre	Floating logs Counting	3–4 mins
Self-propulsion	Swimming-type pattern	Propel self to stations set up around the pool by method most developed	Personal flotation aids if needed Kickboards or flotation aids Large mats as stations	3–4 mins
Steps to submersion & breath control	Steps to readiness for independent submersion with eyes open	Finding sunken treasure	Rings on bottom of pool	2–3 mins
Free play	Group	Whole group on mat, floating, rolling and making a recovery	Large mat	3–4 mins
Goodbye routine	Groups	Actions and song	'Hokey Pokey'	2–3 mins
Exit	Lever body up Deep water exit	Levering body weight up and climbing out independently		

Lesson plan: Preschooler
Age group: 42-48 months
Ability: Experienced
Class day/time: Monday, 11 AM
Number of participants: 4
(parents as observers)

Skills	Focus	Activity	Supporting equipment & songs	Time
Entry	Jumping	Jumping in from edge of the pool with assistance if needed		1–2 mins
Social greeting	Group	'Hello' song Children to greet each other by name	'I'm a Dingle Dangle Scarecrow'	3–4 mins
Floating and balance	Sculling	Floating crocodiles Sculling under an arch	Arch	3–4 mins
Self-propulsion	Swimming-type pattern	Propel self across the pool by method most developed to collect a small ball	Personal flotation aids if needed	3–4 mins
Submersion & breath control	Steps to readiness for independent submersion with eyes open	Swimming down to say hello to self in mirror	Mirror on bottom of pool	2–3 mins
Free play	Group	Ball game in shallow end of pool	Ball	3–4 mins
Goodbye routine	Group	Actions and song	'Hokey Pokey'	2–3 mins
Exit	Hand-walking	Hand-walking from deep end of the pool and levering body weight up to climb out independently		

Teach young swimmers water safety

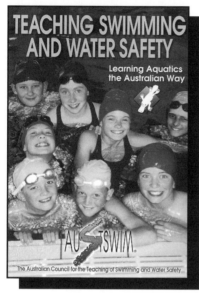

In *Teaching Swimming and Water Safety,* the aquatic education experts at AUSTSWIM provide a proven, effective program for teaching swimming and water safety to children. You will learn how to

- implement important safety procedures;
- use a variety of water familiarization techniques;
- develop floating, propulsion, and deep water skills;
- introduce diving; and
- teach and refine the six common strokes: freestyle, backstroke, breaststroke, butterfly, sidestroke, and survival backstroke.

Highly illustrated and easy to follow, *Teaching Swimming and Water Safety* gives you valuable information on how to safely and effectively teach young swimmers important beginning swimming and water safety skills. Teaching hints and skill processes are included to help you answer questions that come up along the way—it's a resource you will want to refer to again and again.

184 pages • ISBN 0-7360-3251-7 • $18.95 ($27.95 Canadian)

2335